ROYAL TAPESTRY

CHRIS HOWKINS

PUBLISHED BY CHRIS HOWKINS 1985

First Published 1985
© Copyright Christopher Howkins 1985

Printed in England
by Unwin Brothers Limited
at The Gresham Press,
Old Woking, Surrey. GU22 9LH.

ISBN 0 9509105 1 1

To tell of a friend who felt obliged to pay for
an article dropped and broken in a shop would be called
gossip. On the other hand, to tell of Edward IV
feeling obliged to pay 40/- for the damage he and his
Court did to Guildford Friary would be called history.
The difference takes pages to debate but the similarity
only takes one word. They are both stories and that
is all that history is. It is stories about people,
about what they did, how, when, where, why and so forth.
Abbeys, bridges and castles through to yokes and zoos
are the things to look at to illustrate those stories.
They are the tangible remains of other people's lives.

All the stories in this book have a royal connection.
Sometimes monarchs appear in person. Sometimes only
their presence is felt, through legislation, service or
dis-service to the Crown. The great landowners of old
depended upon the success and goodwill of their monarch
in order that they should keep their lands. The lesser
folk depended upon the good fortunes of their landowner for their own and so the royal influence is spread.
Just as the scenes embroidered into the Bayeux Tapestry
create one great picture so the modern images in a
Jean Lurcat tapestry create their theme and so the
varying contents in this book may help illustrate
West Surrey's ROYAL TAPESTRY.

THIS BOOK IS DEDICATED TO

BRIDGET HARPER

WHO DID SO MUCH TO GET IT STARTED

BUT WHO RETIRED AS CURATOR OF CHERTSEY MUSEUM

BEFORE IT WAS COMPLETED.

TRUE OR FALSE

Basically, stories have to be true to be classed as history. This is not as simple as it sounds. Turn to the story of Edward I and Adam de Gurdon and we have a traditional folk tale of which there are several variants. For example, Adam is often based over the Hampshire border, near Crondall. It doesn't matter because the story has been so corrupted to conform to the ideals of chivalry that whatever initiated it has now been lost. As history it has little value but if, however, we were looking into the history of chivalry it might indeed be of value.

All the other references and stories in this book are believed to be true unless otherwise indicated. In a number of cases there are a number of variants and some of course are disputed but the intention was not to produce an authoratative history text book. However, in using popular stories to foster an interest in the world around us there is the danger of blurring fact with fiction. The truth about the "Pilgrims' Way" will never be accepted now. For this reason the stories of King John at the Silent Pool have been omitted deliberately simply because so many people believe them to be true. Nonsense! Martin Tupper made them up.

Tudor Childhood. (for the rich!)

The truth is also difficult to ascertain when contemporary accounts are contradictory. The worst case here is of Mary Tofts. At the time it became a very popular story with many variations. Some of the broadsheets etc. are now in the British Museum. The most painstaking reconstruction seems to be C.J.S.Thomson's "Mysteries of History" (Faber and Gwyer, old but undated).

Some statements were intentionally misleading when made. The Earl of Surrey was surely bluffing when Edward I's Royal Commissioners made their enquiries for the Quo Warranto Writs. Commissioners for Elizabeth I sorted that one out.

This all sounds rather daunting but this is where the fun comes in - and the frustrations. Where there are discrepancies and the story occurs in the Victoria County History then that version has usually been followed.

. . . .

COVER DESIGN : Richard I in single combat with the Sultan Saladin at Babylon, from one of the Chertsey tiles - see separate section.

TITLE PAGE: Rosa alba semi-plena, often sold as the White Rose of York. Surrey was mainly Yorkist. Some of the flowers on this particular bush open in such a way as to show very clearly how they influenced the design of the Tudor rose emblem. Ultimately the rose became the national emblem.

4.

SELECTING THE STORIES

The original intention was to discover whether there was a story from West Surrey to represent every monarch since 1066. In all nearly five hundred stories have been collected to date and so the emphasis has shifted. For the initial selection preference was given to all of those which could be illustrated although this was taken loosely to include such things as plants. There's nothing like growing your own history!

Secondly, attention was turned to variety; to represent a wide scatter of places, a wide range of subject matter for both text and illustration and to try and avoid the book being a repetative assault in black and white. In trying to avoid that I have perhaps invited criticisms for inconsistency! Some of the old favourites have been omitted (no illustration of Claremont!) to make room for some of the lesser known stories. Similarly, some stories continue for reign after reign such as the fortunes of the Earls of Surrey and the repercussions of Forest Law but it was decided not to follow these through as so much else would have to be excluded. Others, such as Fanny Burney's, were too long. It's all been quite a nightmare really !!

Connections with events in our national history occur and it was decided to favour those. Hopefully they will be more meaningful to those readers who know the national context and for others they will be easier to explore further should anyone be so inclined but.....

BEWARE.......in having to introduce that context here in so few words is dangerous. Human motives and actions are never that simple. Modern historians are now reviewing so much and producing fresh insights that many of the statements made here will be challenged. On the whole I have referred to standard text books and these have tended to present the traditional view. Local history enthusiasts have also uncovered much new material which has changed some of the stories and they may well resent the traditional story being used.

THE SOURCES

The full bibliography takes up seven precious pages and has been omitted because most of the entries contain less than what has been pieced together here. It largely comprises guide books to churches, houses, towns etc. Their references were checked wherever possible with the Victoria County History of Surrey. As a quick reference that has been invaluable but it contains many more royal stories than occur in the index. For a longer search use the Surrey Archaeological Collections. These and many more rewarding sources can be found in the Local Studies department of Guildford Library.

Apart from reading there's no substitute for looking and asking. Many of these stories began with an inscription on a church window or a seat or a label on a tree. Others came by simply asking other history enthusiasts, members of local history societies and those invaluable people who take a pride in their village but would never claim to know anything about history. When you think you've got it right someone will come along and tell you otherwise !

TOP illustration - Blackthorn in blossom; Weybridge.
When Henry VIII closed Chertsey Abbey and began preparing to enlarge Oatlands House into a new Palace he took apple, pear and cherry trees from the monks at 6d a load. He bought a further 13,900 crab apple and thorn stocks at 2d per hundred from John Gaddsby of Kingston and William Shore of Mickleham. The thorns were for hedging in the park.

THE CHERTSEY TILES - the only early royal pictures from West Surrey

A hundred years ago Mr. Gumbridge, owner of the site of Chertsey Abbey had a stack of medieval tiles in his garden shed. They had just been excavated from the Abbey site and Dr Mainwaring Shurlock had made careful copies of the designs. Then they were stolen. They haven't been seen since.

The lyon wolde have hym al to rent,
Kyng Richard thenne besyde he glent,
Upon the brest the lyoun he spurnyd,
That al aboute the lyoun turnyd.

This verse and the scene of the combat with the lion come from one of the Romances of Richard the Lionheart. He is shown very much the medieval knight in the design that has been used on the cover. The three leopards on his shield give us his identity, in the days before the leopards were changed to the three lions that we see today. A third study is shown opposite depicting the arrival of a messenger with a letter bearing the baron's seal.

In terms of artwork and technical skill they are among the finest of their age (mid 13th century). They are so fine it was believed they must be French, until the kiln, complete with samples, was found at Chertsey. It also proved the tiles were actually made here and not in London which was possible as the same artist designed the Chapter House floor at Westminster Abbey, laid c.1255.

The identity of that artist is unknown. Professor Lethaby has suggested "Master William", a monk from Winchester, who was the "king's beloved painter". The king was Henry III.

The tiles are of orange red clay with the pictures in white clay which, after glazing, has fired to soft yellow. The pictures were carved in relief on a woodblock which was pressed into the wet clay to leave an indent into which the liquid white clay was poured. That layer is remarkably thin and yet did not separate during firing.

These scenes are on round tiles cut from the centres of square tiles. After firing they had both shrunk equally to ensure a perfect fit when reassembled. That was a supreme achievement of skill and experience, especially in a primitive oven kiln with no controls.

Actual size

A book of Mainwaring Shurlock's drawings is kept at Chertsey Museum where there are also samples in the Abbey displays. Almost opposite is the parish church with some simple tiles on the chancel step. Guildford Museum also displays a sample.

The best displays are in the British Museum and on the Westminster Abbey Chapter House floor.

A NOTE ON FOREST LAW

Forest Law has nothing to do with trees. It's a legal term from the Latin 'foris' meaning outside. The areas under Forest Law were outside the jurisdiction of the Common Law.

Within the 'Forest' the king was the law. English monarchs had enormous areas of this type which made them the most powerful rulers in Europe and the envy of their Continental counterparts. The king's whim was the law. Justice was merely his level of mercy.

William the Conqueror declared all of Surrey to be within his forest but this does not seem to have been enacted because the sheriff does not disappear from the records. He should do because he worked for Common Law. Forest Law was enforced by a royal bailiff.

Resistance to the Law was intense because it was so restrictive. The hunting of deer was obviously outlawed but so was the occupation of tanner in case it promoted poaching. Other animals, such as hares, were protected too. Impeding the hunting or the grazing of the deer was prohibited which meant crops could not be enclosed with obvious results. Nothing could be enclosed without royal sanction, nor new ground cleared nor wood cut. Cottages could not be built and squatters were expelled. Dogs had to be maimed to prevent them hunting. Any contravention of the Law carried very severe penalties.

There were repeated petitions for relief but only gradually in certain areas was it granted and even then there was always the threat of reafforestation. The north west was the last corner to go but even a tiny portion of that, at Virginia Water, is still within Windsor Great Park.

Only snippets from this long and eventful story are included here but will be extended in the next book in this series.

Illustration: Red deer stag in velvet from a photograph lent by Mr. N. Hookins.

Early documentary references to the king's deer are quite specific. Red deer harts were called Cervus with Bissa kept for the hinds. Roe bucks were Capreolus and the does Cheverellus. Buck Fallow deer were Damus and the does or hinds were Dama but this species was probably not introduced until the 12th C.

View from
Pilgrims' Way
near Farnham.
12·6·83

A NOTE ON THE PILGRIMS' WAY

Our understanding of the Pilgrims' Way, as a cross-country route following the North Downs across Surrey, is a fiction concocted in the last century. In truth it is a succession of connecting routes running between the castles, towns and villages along the line of the Downs - a prehistoric route used even before the English Channel was formed.

There is a dearth of documentary evidence for its use. Consequently some writers have reduced its status to a network of local paths but this may be overdoing it. On the occasions when used by soldiers and messengers, their speed suggests that it was clear, direct and well-defined. There is even less evidence for use by pilgrims and they certainly had nothing to do with Chaucer's who followed a totally different route.

There is little archaeological evidence either. A few recovered artifacts indicates only that someone has been there before. Is it coincidence that a new design of "Winchester" window occurs so soon at Effingham beside the route? Further along, at Crondall (just over the Hampshire border) is the only boss of its type outside of Canterbury Cathedral. Is that coincidence? Maybe not but neither do they indicate whole processions of pilgrims.

COUNTY BOUNDARY : The County of Surrey at the time this book begins stretched up to the banks of the River Thames. Since then the expansion of London has forced the boundary southwards several times. Therefore, for the purposes of this book, the current boundary, set in 1974, has been used. The division between east and west has been arbitrary. Basically it follows the A24 London/Worthing road.

TITLE DATES : The main dates are those of the monarch's reign. The single date in brackets is the date of birth.

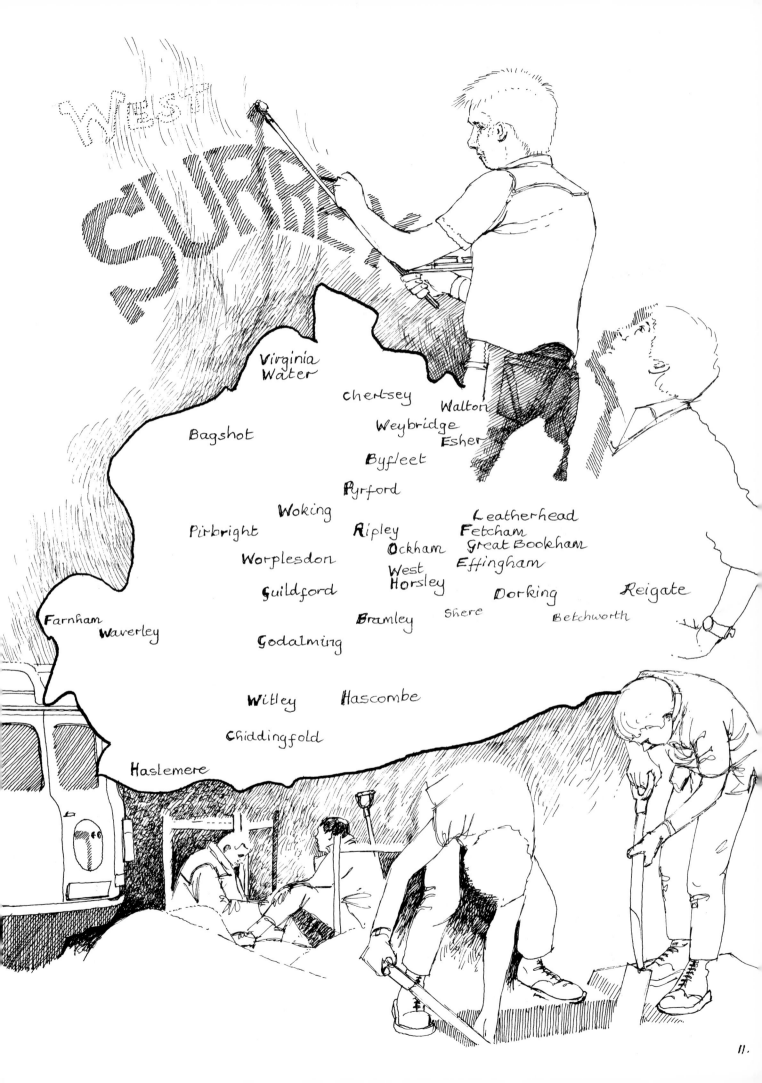

WEST SURREY

Virginia Water

Chertsey   Walton
        Weybridge
Bagshot   Esher
            Byfleet
          Pyrford

        Woking   Leatherhead
Pirbright   Ripley   Fetcham
                Ockham   Great Bookham
    Worplesdon   Effingham
            West
            Horsley
    Guildford   Dorking   Reigate

Farnham   Bramley   Shere   Betchworth
    Waverley

        Godalming

    Witley   Hascombe

Chiddingfold

Haslemere

WILLIAM I   (1027) 1066~1087

How appropriate to be able to begin with one of Surrey's most renowned features - the beautiful rural landscapes. Every year thousands of people, specially from London, search out these scenes from such famous viewpoints as Epsom Downs, Gibbet Hill, Leith Hill, Box Hill and Newlands Corner.

It was from Newlands Corner that this view was sketched. Past here rode William the Bastard, known later as the Conqueror, in 1066. After ravaging London from the South Bank, as far up as Walton-on-Thames, he then reunited his forces near Dorking and journeyed along the Old Road (now called The Pilgrims' Way) to Winchester. This was the capital of Harold's Wessex so it was vital to crush Saxon loyalty there first of all.

Riding along, William must have liked what he saw because he took it all for himself. He declared 'Forest Law' over the whole of Surrey. This remained, in part, for over 600 years until William III in 1694 finally declared in writing that all of Surrey was "now out of the Forest". Today the Crown still holds part of the north-west corner in Windsor Great Park.

To get Windsor, William exchanged it with the Abbot of Westminster for lands at Battersea and Pyrford. He kept back a small area at Pyrford for hunting but at the end of his life he gave that too, "for the health of his soul", to the Abbot. Those lands were exempt from Taxation and Forest Law and so prospered. A later Abbot was criticised for the lavish extravagence of his hospitality there.

Two Surrey holdings were spared the initial ravaging. One was that of Queen Edith, widow of Edward the Confessor. Not until her death did William take her lands, such as Shere, for himself.

The other holding was that of Oswold, a Saxon thane holding land directly from Edward the Confessor and Harold. Somehow Oswold was able to maintain royal favour and did well under William. That would be an interesting story to know!

Beware, translations of Doomsday Book etc. persist in spelling his name the Norman way - Oswald - and thus disguise his Saxon identity.

Owing to Doomsday Book most of our early settlements have a documented history for this period.

At Pyrford may still be visited the small Norman church from those early days. It is the finest of its type in West Surrey, with lots of interest and full of atmosphere.

Pyrford. 81.

WILLIAM II
(1056) 1087 - 1100

The king's most powerful subject in Surrey was Richard de Tonebridge whose family became the famous de Clares. They had sided with Robert, Duke of Normandy, against his father, William I, so William II decided to promote someone over their heads. He chose a landowner from Surrey and Sussex and thereby connected the two counties for the first time. Thus William de Warenne was created first Earl of Surrey and was given Betchworth, Dorking, Fetcham, Reigate and Shere. These had been Queen Edith's lands and therefore inherited personally by the king. Never mind, de Warenne had married into the royal family.

De Warenne built himself a castle at Reigate. This was very convenient for the feud with the de Clares because their castle was next door at Blechingley. Alas, within the year the Earl died.

Fetcham Mill Pond 1974

De Warenne's son, also William, became the second Earl. He was of no use to the king because he sided with the de Clares.

At least the castles of Farnham and Guildford were on the king's side. Places like Loseley, Compton and Worplesdon were held by the son of the great Roger de Montgomery yet even he was not loyal. He joined the de Clares for Duke Robert.

The Lord of such manors as Banstead, Esher, Thames Ditton and Weybridge was a relative, Bishop Odo of Bayeux. He was in prison. The king let him out, hoping to win his favour but he gave Duke Robert another ally.

Eventually the king promised Surrey de-afforestation which was reducing the County to waste and causing much suffering. He promised better laws. He promised less taxes.

He never could keep a promise.

In the end, someone put an arrow in him !

Although the Conqueror had declared all of Surrey to be under Forest Law, this was not fully implemented. Rather than reducing it, William II increased it, by adding his manors of Brookwood, Guildford, Woking and part of Stoke. Even then it was not complete. The County continued to be administered through the civil office of sheriff, rather than a royal bailiff as would otherwise have been the case.

Above:
Fetcham Church, seen through a panel of the lych gate. Parts of the building pre-date the coming of the Normans and thus may have been seen by William de Warenne when he visited his estates. The Normans enhanced and enlarged the building as can be seen from the typical arcade of round-headed arches that still remains inside. This dates from about 1150 and is thus later than William II's reign.

The mill pond can be reached by footpath and lies out in the field at the bottom of the hill across which the modern village is spread.

Right:
John Speede's map of Surrey in 1610 has become well known through modern reproductions. It shows this shield with the arms of William de Warenne, Earl of Surrey.

Godalming
Church and Vicarage
as it is today.

C. Howletts
1985

King William promoted clever people irrespective of rank. He thereby created a "civil service" far ahead of its time. One such person was a minor land owner, Ralph or Rannulph, who from being a clerk in Chancery rose to be the most powerful royal subject. He managed the king's council whether the king was at home or abroad. Nobody from those times has left us a favourable report of him; he seems to have been universally disliked.

He was the stereotyped "baddy" and was known as Flambard in recognition of his trouble-making. He was quite outstanding at devising ways of making money for his king. These ranged from seizing back the damages awarded in the courts to pretending to mount a campaign in Normandy and collecting the 10/- travelling expences off the 20 000 assembled soldiers and then sending them home but keeping the money.

He comes into the story of Surrey when he was made rector of Godalming and settled at Tuesley. Parts of the church at Godalming would have been known to him but the rectory shown in the illustration is not of course that old. His life story is very entertaining but has to be pieced together from many references and short entries.

Thirty four years after the Conquest came Henry I. In lots of ways he was just what was needed. He had the aptitude to weld Saxon with Norman. He was shrewd enough to choose the right people to do it aswell. Thus both the legal system and royal administration were rationalised. From this arose ENGLISH society, with the 12thC. renaissance.

In 1100 Abbot Hugh began rebuilding the important Abbey at Chertsey. It was to increase in importance and to have such royal visitors as King John and the first three Edwards. Now there is little to go and see.

Robert, Duke of Normandy was still being a nuisance. In 1101 the Earl of Surrey took his side and promptly found his Earldom nullified. It was restored the next year when Henry and Robert made peace. That didn't last long. The Earl did, however, learn prudence and remained loyal to the king.

Chertsey's Market Charter was granted to Abbot William in 1129. The current charter came from Elizabeth I in 1599.

HENRY I
(1068) 1100 - 1135

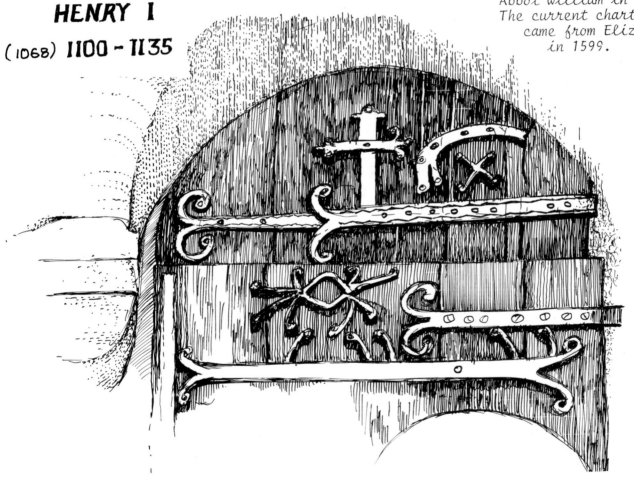

Walk into the tower of St. Peter's Church, Old Woking and the original west door of the church is still in situ, not just the doorway but the wooden door and even the ironwork. Only about forty such doors survive and this is the only one in Surrey.

Just as Henry is known for anglicising the Normans so the style of the ironwork here shows the transition from Scandinavian to English with the great C-shaped hinge in the centre. The top, now alas sawn through, shows its Viking origins. To the right of the Christian cross is the swastika, once the symbol of Thor the High Thunderer but now converted to the service of a new all-powerful god. The zig-zag pattern on the strap hinges may represent the waves lapping the sea monster that encircled the Viking world. The symbolism continues. From evidence on other doors it is conjectured that this represents "Ragnarok", the End of the World, from the Viking poem "Voluspa".

THE FIRST BRIDGE ON THIS SITE
WAS BUILT ABOUT THE YEAR 1100
BY QUEEN MATILDA WIFE OF KING HENRY I
AS AN ACT OF CHARITY IN CONSEQUENCE OF THE
DROWNING OF ONE OF HER MAIDENS AT THE FORD

Cobham Bridge
Part of inscription thereon.

There were new beginnings too in 1128. In that year William Giffard, Bishop of Winchester and former royal chancellor, arranged for certain monks of the new Reformed Orders to enter this country. Thus to Farnham, in his diocese, came Cistercians from L'Aumone in Normandy to found Waverley Abbey. This was the first Cistercian House in Britain. There were seventy five, plus daughter cells, by the 13thC. Of these Waverley founded six. Tintern is often quoted as being the first but it seems Tintern was founded direct from L'Aumone.

These were not isolation hospitals for silent eccentrics in white woollies. They were highly successful centres of business acumen. Although not permitted riches they acquired extensive and valuable estates to make them significant land-owners. They were part of an international organisation that not only wielded influence but disseminated knowledge. When they put their corporate knowledge with their business skills with their edict that "to work is to pray" they made themselves supreme. Whatever they needed they mastered, from textiles to metallurgy. In Britain their contribution was the world's most efficient sheep farming, producing the finest wool. Waverley was part of this, until its final dissolution by Henry VIII in 1536.

WAVERLEY ABBEY

Royal Connections :-

Henry I
Stephen
Richard I
John

Henry III
Edward I
Edward II
Edward III

STEPHEN
(1097) 1135 - 1154

Stephen's reign was largely one of civil war for the crown. It began with both de Clares and de Warennes on the same side — the king's. However, William de Warenne (the third) was fickle.

In 1136 he was on Stephen's side but the next year he was accused of intriguing with Matilda. By 1141 he was back on Stephen's side but was taken prisoner at the Battle of Lincoln. To save himself he quickly swopped loyalties to Matilda but was taken prisoner again when fighting for her at Winchester. He swopped sides again. In 1147 he decided he had better go crusading. The Turks killed him the next year.

Stephen was greatly assisted by his brother, Henry de Blois, Bishop of Winchester and Abbot of Glastonbury. Henry, like so many great landowners in these troubled times, rapidly built castles, usually without royal licence. Henry built seven, including Farnham.

The church at Farnham was given to Waverley Abbey by King Stephen. The king's nephew, Hugh, was Abbot of Chertsey.

At Wanborough the manor was held by Sir Geoffrey de Mandeville. He deserted the king's cause and went over to that of the Empress.

Above:
The south east corner of Farnham Church. It is one of the larger medieval churches in West Surrey. Inside it is lofty and spacious. Outside it has an agreeable sense of space all around it too, despite being adjacent to the town centre. All the approaches are old and attractive.

HENRY II
(1133) 1154 - 1189

Presumably, when Henry de Blois, Bishop of Winchester, built Farnham Castle during the last reign he little imagined that his successors would be using it for over 800 years until 1927, or that it would be taken over for another twenty eight years by the bishops of a new cathedral in what was then the small Norman town of Guildford. That, however, has been the case. It is still in use today.

Certainly Henry II had no such wish. He tried to increase royal power at the expense of the other powerful landowners. Thus he saw the bishop's castles as a threat. Bishop Henry made a mistake. He went to France without royal permission and thereby gave King Henry the chance he was looking for. King Henry seized it. The Sheriff of Hampshire was ordered to destroy the bishop's castles. His expenses are recorded in the Pipe Roll for 1155. It is believed that Farnham was included.

Soon it was rebuilt. The domestic apartments were innovatory in being separate from the keep. Today they show an impressive range of styles and materials illustrating their long history of modification. The blocked chapel arcade (shown above) can be accurately dated to 1254 and by its style can be used to date similar work in Surrey.

Waverley Abbey.

RICHARD I
(1157) 1189 ~ 1199

When the king was the law then the law died with the king. His successor had to swear afresh to uphold the laws and customs of the land. Doubtful agreements were separately reaffirmed. Thus with the accession of Richard I the foreign monks at Waverley felt at risk and petitioned the king.
He reaffirmed their lands and their privileges on 5th September 1189. Four years later he was glad of this when his ransom had to be paid.

Richard the Lionheart was captured on the Third Crusade and the Holy Roman Emperor, Henry VI, demanded a ransom of 150,000 marks. This was equal, it has been calculated, to nearly 50 tons of coinage. It is also said to be about one third of the Gross National Product.

Chests for its collection were set up in churches. Of these one of the finest to survive is in Surrey at Stoke D'Abernon. The churches forfeited their precious metals, even from altars and shrines. Everyone paid.

The Cistercians couldn't comply. They were forbidden to horde such riches by their Rule. They did not escape however. Instead they were charged to yield one year's wool harvest. Being Europe's foremost sheep farmers, this was a substantial demand. The ransom was paid. Richard returned in 1194.

With the accession of Richard the people promptly petitioned for the release of Surrey from Forest Law. To this he agreed except for the lands to the north of the Hog's Back and west of the River Wey. This agreement cost 200 marks; an unfortunate precedent.

The north west corner became the Surrey Bailiwick of Windsor Forest, presided over by the Bailiff, except for Egham, Thorpe and Chertsey which belonged to Chertsey Abbey. The rest of Surrey was presided over by the County Sheriff.

Forest Law was a major restriction on the development of Surrey. King Richard doesn't seem to have honoured his charter of release. Neither did John. In fact his inclinations were to reafforest. The Knights of the Shire persuaded him otherwise but at the cost of 200 marks plus 100 marks to reaffirm Richard's Charter. That was in 1205. In 1207-8 Surrey was charged 500 marks which is presumed to have been in addition to the previous charges. Such abuses **led** to Magna Carta.

JOHN (1167) 1199-1216

John's fame, at the time, was for his energy and for his horsemanship.

Coming from Normandy for his coronation, he landed at Shoreham on 25th May. He left the next day and was in London the day after. He was always on the move. He changed his base two or three times a fortnight. Trying to keep up with him was an exhausting nightmare for the royal court.

His most frequently used base was Guildford. He was there at least nineteen times. His Christmas celebrations there in 1201 were noted for their "extraordinary splendour".

In 1208 he broke his journey from Southampton to Guildford in order to celebrate Easter with the monks at Waverley Abbey. He arrived on 2nd April and did not leave until the 5th, (Easter Saturday). During that time something intriguing happened..............

waverley.

..........John was having one of his disputes and all church property had been seized. When he left Waverley he ordered the release of the rents and possessions of William de Broadwater, Priest at Waverley, that he might continue building up the Abbey at his own expense. Now how did they persuade John to do that?

He wasn't a friend for long. Within two years the Abbot had to flee by night because the Cistercian Order had refused the king 'improper' payments. The Abbey's privileges were withdrawn. All personel scattered but were forbidden to leave the country. Cistercians from abroad were refused entry.

Another two years and John is at them again. This time he forced them to resign their property to him.

MAGNA CARTA :

NO FREEMAN SHALL BE ARRESTED, OR IMPRISONED, OR DISPOSSESSED, OR OUTLAWED, OR EXILED, OR IN ANY WAY RUINED, EXCEPT BY LAWFUL JUDGEMENT OF HIS PEERS OR BY THE LAW OF THE LAND.

Clause 39.

......the most famous clause from our most famous document. The signing of Magna Carta by King John at Runnymede is the only event in the history of Surrey to be of great importance, not only nationally but internationally with its usage by the 17thC. colonists of New England.

They misunderstood it, as did the British parliamentarians when using it against the Stuarts. It was not intended to be a Bill of Human Rights but was primarily concerned with specific grievances. It did formalise some fundamental principles (such as clause 39) and highlight the emerging idea that royal power would now have to take account of public interest.

It did not provide the means to fulfil more. This was later rectified by the Provisions of Oxford (1258) and the Provisions of Westminster (1259). Thus England became the first European country to have a written constitution.

Contrary to what is often said, King John DID sign Magna Carta. He did not write his name on it but he did affix his royal seal. That signed it because in both medieval and classical Latin "signum" meant a mark, whether name, cross or seal. (correction to my Doorstep Book, p.28 !)

Neither was King John the first ruler to be coerced in this way. The Emperor Frederick Barbarossa had a similar problem with the Lombards in 1183 and so did Alphonso VII in Leon, Northern Spain, in 1188. The old social orders were changing in Europe.

The Pope, Innocent III, was slower to change and was outraged by Magna Carta because he was overlord of John and of England since England had been enfiefed to the papacy since 1213. It was also contrary to feudal law because the barons had been both executors and judges in their own case.

Thus Innocent III annulled Magna Carta, quoting Jeremiah: "I have set thee over the nations and over the kingdoms to root out and to destroy, to build and to plant."

Interestingly, his own agent in England, Pandulf, had signed Magna Carta. Despite the annulment being perpetual, the Papal Legate, Guala, was to seal a revised version after the death of Innocent.

Revised versions were issued in 1216, 1217 and 1225. The last became the basis of English Law. Magna Carta, however, didn't solve the immediate problem and the struggle went on.

.....The Pope sent for the Archbishop of Canterbury and thereby removed the main moderating influence between the king and his barons. They promptly invited Louis, Dauphin of France, to invade and depose John. He came that winter. A storm dispersed John's fleet as it prepared to intercept the French so John waited on land in Kent. Behind him were the Surrey castles on the king's side. So was the Pope.

When Louis arrived John fled. Leaving Kent, he hurried through Surrey to Winchester with Louis in pursuit, taking the castles along the way. Blechingley was no problem as the de Clares, Richard and Gilbert had both been excommunicated with other barons, by the Pope, to try and curtail their rebelliousnous. Reigate castle was de Warenne's and he was for the king but nevertheless his castle surrendered. Guildford was a royal castle but that too was taken without force. Farnham surrendered.

Magna Carta Memorial
Runnymede.

De Warenne changed to Louis' side to get his castle back. Then John lost the support of the Pope who went and died. Next John died. Louis should have been secure; he had already won over the Eastern Counties, but the French and the barons didn't trust each other. Louis' cause crumbled especially as he had to return to France for a few months.

On 27th March 1217 Gilbert de Clare made peace with the Crown. On 16th April de Warenne did the same. Farnham Castle had been taken back by the Earl of Pembroke in March. This Earl was Regent for the new king, Henry III, who was only nine. He brought the boy king to Kingston to begin negotiations with Louis. Finally, at Lamberth, on 11th September 1217 the treaty was concluded. On 14th September Louis was assured safe conduct to leave the realm and five days later, the same for his men, waiting at Merton. It was a good start to a new reign which would run for over half a century.

HENRY III
(1207) 1216 - 1272

Henry III is well known for his wars with Simon de Montfort, resulting in what is often claimed to be the first English parliament. Surrey saw none of the conflict but it did see Simon and Gilbert de Clare go through in a mighty hurry.

Already weary from their journey from the Welsh Marches (other de Clare country) they were at Reading on June 29th 1263. The next day they were at Guildford and at Reigate the day after. They were very intent on seizing Dover. As far as we know from Reading to Guildford they would have had to cross open country and so the speed is all the more remarkable. The main road was used from Guildford. We now call that the Pilgrims' Way.

Simon's route in winter; view from the Pilgrims' Way, near Ranmore.

Guildford was one of the main centres for Henry III, making it the most important place in Surrey. He extended the castle into a grand palace, now just a few ruins around the keep. Below these 'Castle Arch' still stands. This was probably the work of his Master Mason, John of Gloucester, about 1256. Then too he had his gardens made, complete with a cloister of marble columns. In 1268 the queen's garden was made. That was the job of the Court painter, William Florentyn, who was paid 6d per day for his artistry in this matter. The queen was able to continue to enjoy her garden after her husband's death because she then held Guildford Castle in dower. The recorded details of the gardens are precious because so few records of medieval gardens have survived. Probably broom (left) was grown because it was the emblem of the Plantagenets.

Below the castle, on the river, the king had a fulling mill from 1251 to 1267 which is one of the earliest recorded. Guildford cloth was already fine enough for the king who purchased 'Chalons of Guildford' in 1252.

Stories for both Henry, and his brother-in-law, Simon de Montfort, come from the history of Waverley Abbey.

The prestige of the Cistercian Order is emphasised for us today by Henry's wish to become an Associate of the Order. Thus in December 1225 he braved the winter journey and travelled to Waverley Abbey. There, with great solemnity he was admitted as an Associate on the 17th.

In 1245 it was the turn of his sister, Eleanor, to visit. She arrived with husband Simon, two sons and three of her handmaidens. Such a female intrusion required an Indulgence from the Pope.

By this time Henry was none too popular at Waverley. He needed finances for the wars in Gascony but the Order had refused to pay.

Thus in 1242 the king ordered the Archbishop of York to persuade them otherwise. This he tried but failed. Consequently the Cistercians were banned from leaving the country to attend their General Chapter, (Their International Conference). In 1244 they were still sticking to their rights, and so were banned from selling their wool which was their main source of income. In 1256 they continued about their business and sent their representatives to the General Chapter. On returning they were seized until they paid a 'passage toll'. Many couldn't and so had to sell even the clothing they wore.

"Castle Arch" Guildford.

Farnham Castle – exit from
the keep.

EDWARD I
(1239) 1272 – 1307

Once upon a time there was a tall, dark, handsome prince who was brave and strong and a noble leader. He sallied forth from his castle at Guildford one day and journeyed westwards towards the castle at Farnham. There, it was said, ruled an evil baron called Adam de Gurdon who had soldiered for the prince's wicked uncle, Simon de Montfort.

The noble prince did meet this Adam in the woods by chance. Both were far from the safety of their castles but this bothered not the noble prince. He challenged Adam there and then. The seasoned soldier smiled upon the youth and into single combat they did go.

The noble prince, famed for length of arm and leg and for the strength therein did induce the evil Adam to submit. He took him as his prisoner back to Guildford town.

The people said there'd be a hanging. The prince, with face so lean and stern, did look upon the prisoner and saw not an enemy to kill but a knight with virtues he could use. Thus it happened that Adam de Gurdon was taken into the prince's service.

. . . .

This is a traditional tale found with several variations but which remains unsubstantiated. Whatever incident inspired it has now been lost and the story wrapped in the ideals of chivalry.

. . . .

Edward I spent much of his youth at Guildford Castle with his parents and with his beloved Eleanor of Castile whom he married in 1254. She was ten and he was fifteen. In 1290 she died and he took as his second wife, Margaret of France. After his coronation he continued to visit Guildford and aided the Friary with timber, fuel, donations etc.

Walking round Guildford, there is much to remind us of Edward I, even if he would have difficulty recognising it. His castle survives albeit in fragments. The Friary has been swept away but is commemorated in the name of the shopping complex on the site. The king himself is commemorated with Queen Eleanor on the sundial erected on the end of the Tunsgate buildings. The modern law courts (illustrated) remind us that Edward I reorganised the law court system.

Edward I is thought to have been the last monarch to travel from north to south in Surrey until the reign of Elizabeth I. There must have been a good road. He was, for example, at Witley in 1294 and held court there in 1305, possibly on the site of the present 'White Hart'. His queen, Margaret, held Witley by 1313.

The road probably ran to Shoreham for the crossing to Normandy. After King John lost Normandy the port and the road lost their importance. Henceforth traffic was to go to the west of Surrey to Southampton or to the east to the Cinque Ports. Surrey, however, being convenient to both these routes and to such important places as London and to some extent Winchester, remained a desirable place in which to live.

A famous story from English history comes from the Earl of Surrey at this time. It was de Warenne who threw his sword on the table declaring that just as his ancestors had won their lands by the sword so he would now defend them with the sword. History proves his claim ill-founded but his concern was real enough. It arose from Edward's quo warranto writs enquiring into the entitlement of the landowners to their lands and franchises. Those royal commissioners must have been most unpopular!

The development of Surrey was still restricted by Forest Law and Edward wanted to extend this. It wasn't like the old days though. The barons were now united in a parliament with a new strength. There were enquiries and commissioners and court hearings. Agreements were reached and broken. The Pope still did his anulling act but in the end Edward failed to win. The law of the Forest Charters won, not the will of the king. The severity of Forest Law was reduced with a new Forest Ordinance.

From among the modern housing at the east
end of Byfleet village, Mill Lane follows
the River Wey to a slight rise whereon is
built Byfleet Manor. It is the latest in
a succession of manor houses here and dates
from the 1686 rebuilding for Anne of Denmark,
queen to James I and last royal owner.

EDWARD II
(1284) 1307–1327

Further up the Wey, at Guildford, Edward was causing consternation at the Friary. Dominican brothers were to be ousted in favour of Dominican sisters in order that Edward could cheaply fulfil the wish of his mother to found a nunnery.

The Bishop of Winchester was persuaded to support the cause and so the Pope was petitioned by letter and envoy but all to no avail. The brothers kept their Friary.

Five years later Edward visited the Friary and donated 8/- for a day's food to each of the 24 brothers.

The first royal owner remains unknown as back in Saxon times Byfleet was given to Chertsey Abbey. By the reign of Edward II it was obviously used by royalty as shown by the address on many of his documents. These early times are commemorated in the modern street names such as "Edward II Avenue" and "Gaveston Close". Piers Gaveston, one of the king's notorious favourites, was given the right to have a rabbit warren here and so presumably had been given the manor previously. He's also recalled by "Gaveston Road" at Leatherhead, where their friend Randolph was given lands. That's now corrupted to Randall as in "Randall Farm Lane", "Randall Park", "Randalls Road" etc.

EDWARD III
(1312) 1327 - 1377

Little florets in bright blue from the Borage, picked for salads.

"Eat Borage
Get Courage"

It has been suggested as one of the plants chosen to brighten the new garden made at Henley Park especially for the visit of the king and queen in 1343.

It is an annual that flowers quickly and so is a high contender to have been chosen. Considerable notice of the royal visit must have been given because the new garden sounds like a major undertaking. It required a drawbridge from the hall. There was a viewing tower and maybe a fishpond. Again Surrey provides some of the rare details of medieval gardens. The Borage is still in cultivation but those royal gardens have not survived.

The nuns at Dartford Priory in Kent were not a wealthy household and so the prioress must have been well pleased to receive the advowson of Witley church from the king. The church was appropriated to them too.

However, the prioress had no wish to be caught out. She doubted whether these dealings would remain valid and so wrote to the Pope for confirmation. He duly sent a new licence in October 1395.

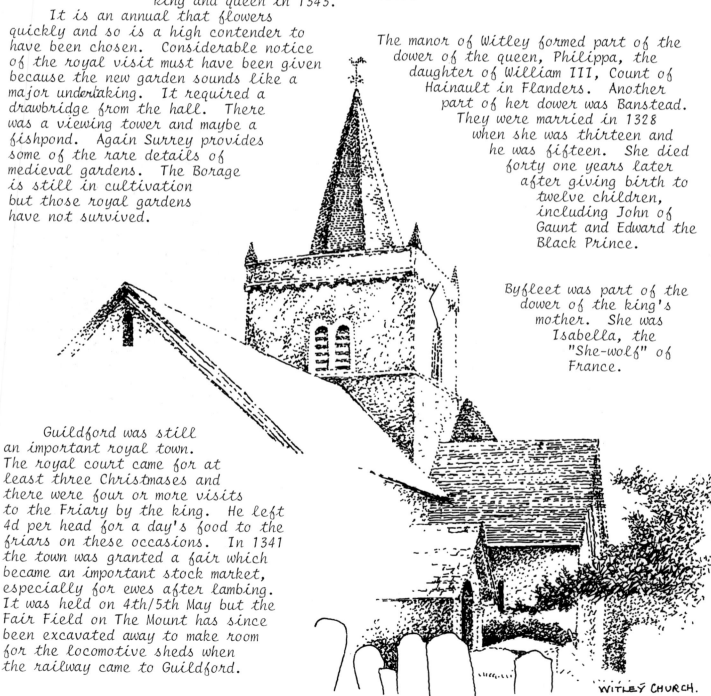

The manor of Witley formed part of the dower of the queen, Philippa, the daughter of William III, Count of Hainault in Flanders. Another part of her dower was Banstead. They were married in 1328 when she was thirteen and he was fifteen. She died forty one years later after giving birth to twelve children, including John of Gaunt and Edward the Black Prince.

Byfleet was part of the dower of the king's mother. She was Isabella, the "She-wolf" of France.

Guildford was still an important royal town. The royal court came for at least three Christmases and there were four or more visits to the Friary by the king. He left 4d per head for a day's food to the friars on these occasions. In 1341 the town was granted a fair which became an important stock market, especially for ewes after lambing. It was held on 4th/5th May but the Fair Field on The Mount has since been excavated away to make room for the locomotive sheds when the railway came to Guildford.

WITLEY CHURCH.

At last, a face to put to a story. It comes from the memorial brass to Walter Frilende in Ockham Church. It is not a portrait despite its distinctiveness. The craftsman who took up his burin and gouged out a priest is highly unlikely to have ever met him in real life. Walter was the "King's Clerk" which might mean he was only a civil servant in the Exchequer. Anyway the King knew him and respected him and so did his patron the Earl of Stafford. That was Ralph de Stafford who married a local lady in 1347 and paid for relief of her lands, including Ockham. Two years later and Walter was instated as rector. He was still in Minor Orders and had to be ordained as a priest later. This may scandalise some readers today but was not unusual then. Even the ceremony for making Thomas à Becket the Archbishop of Canterbury had to be immediately preceded by one to make him a bishop first!

It is very rare that we know who built our medieval churches or even who paid for them. However at Ockham we know that Walter Frilende paid for the north aisle to be demolished and rebuilt as the Chapel of St. Margaret. Today we can still walk into it through the arches illustrated; the same arches that Walter knew.

The swastikas on his vestment were ancient symbols of goodness, used for over 4,000 years by Hindus, Red Indians, Buddhists etc. It was a secret symbol of the Christians in the Catacombs.

RICHARD II

(1367) 1377 - 1399

Richard was the GRANDSON of his predecessor. His father, Edward the Black Prince, never became king because he died in 1376. The Black Prince figures for many years in the history of Byfleet.

It is West Horsley, however, that leads us into the story of Richard II. Preserved in a north chancel window of the church is a small panel of stained glass inscribed with the name of Sir James Berners. The knight (sketched here) is shown as a donor, kneeling on a chequered tile floor like a chess board.

This knight was taken out of play by the king.

Sir James was one of Richard's favourites and acted as advisor. His advice was not impartial and he was blamed for the insurrection of 1388. For this he was arrested and executed on Tower Hill.

Thus the manor of West Horsley was forfeited to the Crown but in 1393 Richard relented and returned it to Sir James's widow and heirs.

Sir James had been accused of taking advantage of the king's youth. Richard was only ten when he was crowned. Thus the country was governed initially by a Council of Regency.

These noble gentlemen let him down in 1381 during the Peasants' Revolt. If teen-agers are sometimes difficult to understand today they have not changed all that much for in 1381 Richard was fourteen and went out alone in London to meet the thousands of massed rioters. They were demanding an audience with the king and that was exactly what he gave them. It worked. They listened. Agreements were made and peace was restored. That was very short lived. The Council immediately rescinde the pardons Richard had granted. They hanged the leaders and blackened Richard's name.

The Earl of Surrey and Sussex was appointed head of the Commission to deal with the revolt in his two Counties. Offenders were taken to the County Gaol, Guildford Castle, and when that was full, to the castles at Lewes and Arundel.

Much grievance was held against the Abbot of Chertsey and so he had problems on his Abbey estates at Chertsey, Chobham, Egham and Thorpe. The estate workers got to the manorial records and destroyed them. At Guildford the rioters got to the town's charters and destroyed many of those too.

The Earl went on to become one of the Lords Appellant, asserting the judicial supremacy of Parliament. For this impertinence the king had him beheaded in 1397.

Abbey Fore-field, Chertsey. The football pitch was once the Abbey's western precinct.

Richard's contribution to the history of Byfleet introduces another national figure. He needed a literate servant to be Clerk of Works and he chose the man recently restored to favour after his release from the Tower.

It was the man who loved the fresh beauty of daisies, Geoffrey Chaucer, who later wrote "The Canterbury Tales". He seems to have held the office for less than two years but it remains important simply because his signature has survived on one of the documents. That document relates to work at the royal manor of Byfleet.

Daisies have retained their popularity with the British. In this century they were used in schools during the patriotic celebrations of Empire Day (May 24th) when the yellow centre represented Great Britain and the white petals represented all the countries of the Empire.

With the so-called "Pilgrims' Way" going through Surrey, Chaucer's "Canterbury Tales" are too often associated with it. His pilgrims travelled to Canterbury from London not Winchester. Pilgrims did use this prehistoric route as is reflected in the histories of many of the adjacent churches. Archaeological evidence can perhaps be seen at the ruined chapel of St.Catherine, overlooking Guildford. Looking in at the north west corner (illustrated) one sees a stairway going up through the wall to an upper doorway. This once gave access to some sort of walkway. Perhaps this was to enable the circulation of processions and an easier view of the altar when the chapel was used by larger crowds than those for which it was designed.

Turning to Witley again, it is now held by Mundina Davos who was the king's nurse. She was married to Rauf who was the king's tailor. Meanwhile, Pirbright was being disemparked. In Woking Park by contrast, there were developments. Richard might have been responsible for rebuilding the manor house.

The Peasants" Revolt arose out of the Poll Tax. This was the taxation of all individuals over fourteen years of age. Originally introduced in 1222, it was levied again in 1377, 1379 and 1381 but was so widely evaded that commissioners were sent out in 1381 to collect arrears and this sparked the revolt. The adult population of Surrey according to this census was 12,622.

HENRY IV
(1367) 1399 - 1413

Stormy day, Worplesdon.

This was our first king since 1066 to be born in England of English parents. His claim to the throne and his efforts to keep it make a complicated but absorbing story.

Just as his predecessor had to contend with the Peasants' Revolt so Henry IV had to contend with the Lollards. They campaigned for religious and then constitutional reform but their greatest contribution was that they preached in English instead of Latin and they popularised Wycliffe's English Bible.

By attacking wealth and worldliness they made enemies of both Church and State. In Surrey they were not very active but Worplesdon provides a link with one of their most important leaders, Sir John Oldcastle.

Sir John was Lord Cobham (the Kent Cobham not the Surrey Cobham) and his line held the right of advowson for Worplesdon church. He was one of the few Lollards to be drawn from the important landowners.

In the year that the crown passed from Henry IV to Henry V Oldcastle was arrested and convicted of heresy against his former friend, now the new king. Off he went to the Tower but maintained the tradition of escaping. He then organised an unsuccessful revolt and had to go into hiding. It was three years before they caught him - and executed him.

****

Henry IV married Mary de Bohun, thereby bringing into the history of West Surrey another family of national importance. She was co-heiress of Humphrey de Bohun, Earl of Hereford and Essex. The Surrey connection is that part of her dower was the manor of Walton. The present manor house is medieval but of a later date.

A more intriguing story comes from Guildford where the royal family lodged at the Friary on February 12th 1403. When they left the king paid 40/- in compensation for the damage they caused to the house, its contents and the gardens. What did they get up to ?

HENRY V
(1387) 1413 - 1422

Henry V, the great showman, had unusual good luck, especially for an English King. He is better remembered for his unlikely triumph at Agincourt than for starting the Hundred Years War to fulfil Edward III's claim to the French throne. Even Agincourt seems unrecorded in West Surrey. Despite numerous advertisements and a long search, no town or village has proudly drawn my attention to any connection. Betchworth is the nearest.

Here lived the king's surgeon, present at Agincourt. He left money in his will for the "reparation and amendment" for that part of the church "in which my fader and moder ben buried". (Their brass inscription memorial was obstructed from view at the time of writing, May 1985).

Farmyard geese are the other reminder. From each of these the County Sheriff had to collect six wing feathers to flight the arrows of the archers who were to win the day. What an administrative headache that must have been !

Sir John Stanley of Henley Park provides another connection with Henry V because the king sent him to Ireland, where he died. Among other things he was the first Keeper of the Royal Parks.

Productions of Shakespeare's "Henry V" provide an irregular reminder although perhaps we should also remember that both Shakespeare's house and the Globe Theatre were then within the County boundary that went up to the banks of the Thames.

Betchworth
1985

HENRY VI

**(1421)
1422~1461
1470~1471**

Come, now towards Chertsey
    with your holy load,
Taken from Paul's to be interred there;
And still, as you are weary of the weight,
Rest you, whilst I lament King Henry's corse.

Shakespeare: Richard III, Act I, scene ii.

The double dates at the top of this entry speak for themselves of these troubled times. The Wars of the Roses contributed comparatively little to the County's history; Reginald Bray, who occurs later, has yet to negotiate the final peace by arranging a marriage between the two Houses. Surrey was mainly for the House of York. The main Lancastrian influence was through the Staffords, who had inherited lands from the de Clares (see Ockham).

This grim stone face, now in Weybridge Museum, once stared down from the Chapter House of Chertsey Abbey. He would have seen the comings and goings on the day the body of the murdered king was brought for burial from the Tower of London. Henry VI, our most Christian king, according to some appraisals, came to one of the greatest Abbeys to rest in peace. Ironically the Dissolution of the Monasteries destroyed that peace and he had to be moved. It now seems generally agreed that he was moved to Windsor but some authorities prefer London. He was the only monarch to be buried in Surrey.

One of his more loyal subjects was Nicholas Hussey, County Sheriff, who lived at Hascombe Manor (opposite). He had also served the king as Lieutenant of Guisnes Castle and as Victualler of Calais. In the reign of the next king he was accused of not paying his dues since the accession. However, that problem was solved and Nicholas was pardoned in 1467. As a younger son, Nicholas was doing well. He got his lands simply because his elder brother was outlawed and forfeited his rights in 1454. Even so, his manor must have been extremely remote for a County official. Perhaps there were days when he felt that was an advantage!

Hascombe Manor, now known as Hascombe Place, is not the original house but the string of fish ponds survives. One can be seen behind the church. The house site is not open to the public but can be seen from the footpath leading up from the right hand side of the village pub.

Hascombe
Place
14-4-85.
C. Hawkins.

39.

EDWARD IV
(1442)
1461~1470   1471~1483

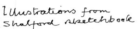
Illustrations from
Shalford sketchbook

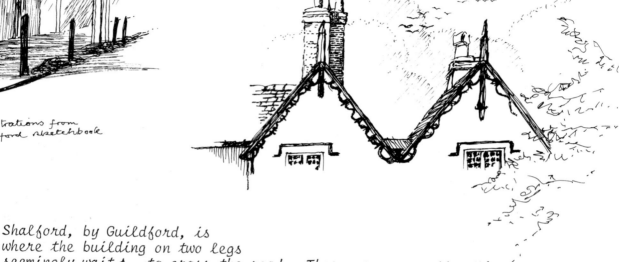

Shalford, by Guildford, is
where the building on two legs
seemingly waits   to cross the road.   There are many attractive
gabled cottages but by the church the old stocks are a reminder of grimmer
times.

　　　Back in the reign of Edward IV the manor of Shalford was held by John,
Lord Clifford.   He was not on Edward's side during the Wars of the Roses and
so when he was killed at Ferrybridge his lands were seized (he was attainted
so that his heirs could have no claim to them).   In his place, the king
granted Shalford to one of his servants, an Usher, called Nicholas Gaynesford.
With the eventual accession of Richard III it was all change again when it was
　　　　　　　　　　Gaynesford's turn to be attainted.

　　　Over at Henley Park on the other side of Guildford, Edward made
another appointment that would come into the news again with the
reign of Richard III. The king appointed his brother-in-law, Sir
Thomas St. Leger, as Keeper of the Royal Park.

　　　Brother George, Duke of Clarence, was given Witley in 1464
but was sent abroad the following year.   In 1478 he was
murdered as a traitor (supposedly drowned in a barrel of
Malmsey Wine). His name appears on a fragment of inscribed
　　　　　　　　　　stone preserved in Witley church.
　　　　　　　　　　It was never finished and shows us how
　　　　　　　　　　the text was scratched out ready for
　　　　　　　　　　　　cutting. It reads- "Georgii
　　　　　　　　　　　　ducis Clarence dominii de
　　　　　　　　　　　　Wytle ac fratis Edwardi IV
　　　　　　　　　　　　regis Angliae et Franchiae".

THE FRIARY

Edward IV came in 1479 to stay in Guildford Friary - then a monastery, not a shopping centre of course! There he treatied with Burgundy on 16th August.

By that Treaty his four year old daughter, Anne was to one day marry Philip (then only fourteen months old), the son of Maximilian and Mary of Burgundy.

This did not come to pass. Instead, Anne eventually married the Thomas Howard who became Duke of Norfolk and Earl of Surrey.

Philip married Joanna of Spain and fathered Charles V, King of Spain and the Netherlands and Emperor of Germany. It was this powerful ruler who was beseiging the pope when our Henry VIII needed the pope's support over his proposed divorce of Catherine of Aragon. The Pope didn't dare give it because Catherine was Charlie's Aunt.

-- -- -- --

The village of Pirbright has seen many changes. In early times it had a royal park until Richard II disparked it. Later the manor came into the hands of Cecily, daughter of Ralph Neville, Earl of Westmorland. Her son held it of her and he was Edward IV. Due to him, much of the land was emparked again and his first Keeper was Sir Thomas Bourchier.

Pirbright is still an attractive village today with a pond on the green and ducks to enjoy or a game of cricket to watch. Brick and tile cottages add colour through the trees and up at the church Stanley of Livingstone fame is buried.

41.

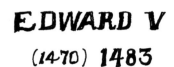

EDWARD V
(1470) 1483

Ockham Church
The Stafford Knots.

Edward V was king for eleven weeks. His reign lasted from 9th April until 25th June. He was twelve years old. Obviously he didn't have time to be a great king but he is one whom many readers will have at least vaguely heard of, as one of "The Princes in the Tower"- that great unsolved mystery from English history.

That story involves Henry Stafford, Duke of Buckingham and he has connections with West Surrey. He was lord of the manor of Ockham and patron of the church. Inside the church there is still a reminder of those days and the Stafford connection.

One of the devices of the family was the "Stafford Knot" and this can still be seen around the border of a south chancel window (as illustrated). It is fashioned in stained glass of a greenish colour which indicates that it came from the famous glass centre of Chiddingfold in Surrey. Little of that glass has survived in Surrey churches. .

Henry Stafford was married as a child to the queen's younger sister, Catherine Woodville, in the hope of allying him to the Yorkist cause. Henry, however, grew to be a staunch Lancastrian, supporting Richard, Duke of Gloucester.

So it was, in 1483, when Prince Edward was being brought to London to be crowned Edward V the group was intercepted at Stony Stratford. The interceptors were his uncle, Richard, Duke of Gloucester, and Henry Stafford, Duke of Buckingham.

Removing the prince from his Yorkist guards they took him themselves to the Tower of London to await his coronation. Gloucester was confirmed as Protector of the Realm and Buckingham got the greater power that he was seeking.

Buckingham worked against Edward in favour of Gloucester. He won over London to his cause with a speech in the Guildhall and a few days later, on 26th June, delivered to Gloucester a petition from the Lords and Commons inviting him to take the crown. Gloucester took it.

At his coronation he became Richard III with Buckingham acting as Great Chamberlain.

RICHARD III (1452) 1483-1485

The previous story continues with Buckingham ceasing to support Richard. The reason for this is no longer very clear. Anyway, there was a movement to try and free the Princes in the Tower - Edward and Richard of York.

When it was realised that they had probably been murdered the exiled Henry Tudor was invited to return from Brittany and overthrow Richard. Henry set sail. The rebels plotted and planned.

C. Hawkins
9·6·84

The insurrection was planned by the southern Counties for 18th October when indeed the resurgents met in Guildford. The County leader wasn't present. He was Sir Thomas St. Leger of Field Place at Compton, near Guildford (sketched above).
Unfortunately for them, Kent had bungled it. They rose too early, before 10th, and thereby warned Richard. On 15th Buckingham was declared a rebel. He was betrayed and caught in the West Country. He was executed at Exeter. His wife, the king's sister, was the Duchess of Exeter.
The lands of Sir Thomas were confiscated by the king, including Field Place. This was then given to William Mistelbroke in recognition of his loyalty. History doesn't record what sort of reception the villagers gave him when he arrived.
Eventually Henry Tudor confronted Richard on Bosworth Field and defeated him. Richard became our first king to die in battle since Harold at Hastings.

N.B. Field Place is NOT open to the public.

43.

HENRY VII
(1457)
1485 ~ 1509

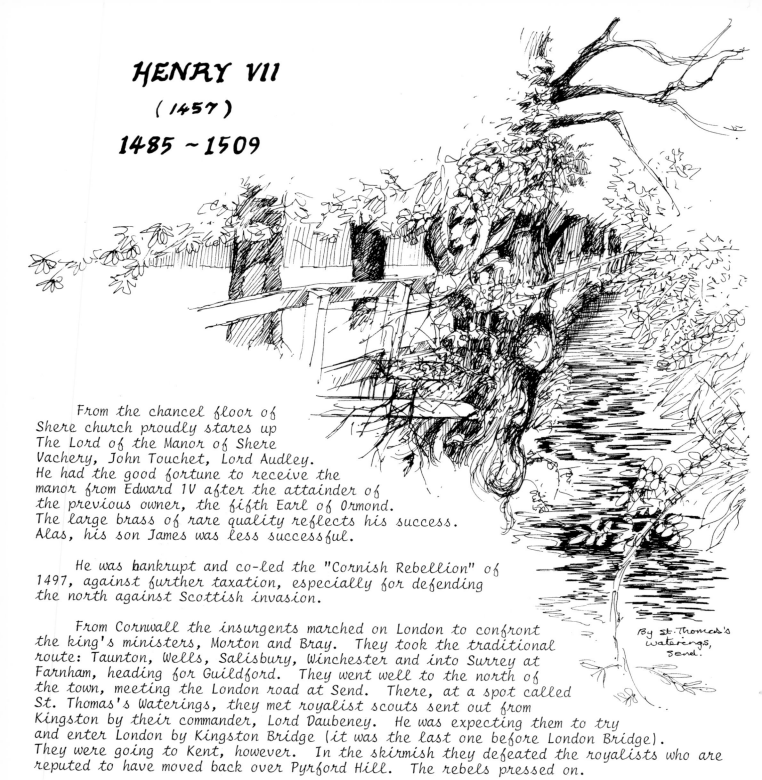

By St. Thomas's
Waterings,
Send.

From the chancel floor of
Shere church proudly stares up
The Lord of the Manor of Shere
Vachery, John Touchet, Lord Audley.
He had the good fortune to receive the
manor from Edward 1V after the attainder of
the previous owner, the fifth Earl of Ormond.
The large brass of rare quality reflects his success.
Alas, his son James was less successful.

He was bankrupt and co-led the "Cornish Rebellion" of
1497, against further taxation, especially for defending
the north against Scottish invasion.

From Cornwall the insurgents marched on London to confront
the king's ministers, Morton and Bray. They took the traditional
route: Taunton, Wells, Salisbury, Winchester and into Surrey at
Farnham, heading for Guildford. They went well to the north of
the town, meeting the London road at Send. There, at a spot called
St. Thomas's Waterings, they met royalist scouts sent out from
Kingston by their commander, Lord Daubeney. He was expecting them to try
and enter London by Kingston Bridge (it was the last one before London Bridge).
They were going to Kent, however. In the skirmish they defeated the royalists who are
reputed to have moved back over Pyrford Hill. The rebels pressed on.

John Touchet had died six years before and so did not see his son go past Shere.
As a benefactor for Royalist support he probably wouldn't have approved. It must have
been an impressive sight though. There were reckoned to be 15,000 rebels but this is
thought to be exaggerated and many must have dropped back along the way. Even so, it's
odd that Daubeney couldn't keep proper track of them.

Many more must have dropped out when they reached Kent because contrary to
expectation the people of Kent declined to join them. The remainder went on to
camp on Blackheath and be defeated. James was beheaded for his treason.

The next year Henry VII ironically granted James's manor to James's critic -
Sir Reginald Bray. James was able to keep certain rights until his execution.
The Bray family are still present in the district today and those who have spanned the
years between have their memorials in Shere church.

John Touchet. his brass.
Sketched from
E. Hawkins 11.5.85

It was Reginald Bray who is said to have pulled the crown of England from under a Hawthorn bush on Bosworth Field. Lord Stanley placed it on the head of Henry Tudor to the cries of "Henry! King Henry! King Henry!"

The crown and the thorn on a fragment of 15thC. glass in Witley church reminds us of that. Witley was inherited by Bray in 1495 on the death of his uncle, Jasper Tudor. At Henry's coronation Bray was made a Knight of the Bath and a few months later made Keeper of the Royal Parks at Guildford, Henley and Pirbright.

He was a highly talented man. Not only was he a worthy soldier, courtier and politician but also an inspired architect, leaving us such soaring glories as Henry VII's Chapel at Westminster Abbey and St. George's Chapel at Windsor.

HENRY VIII
(1491) 1509~1547

This monarch did more than any other to create the Surrey we know today. By closing the monasteries he changed the social services. By redistributing their lands he created new patterns of tenure and usage. The break with Rome encouraged an independent national identity yet admitting the influence of the Renaissance. His church reforms led to the buildings and their services taking on the forms we know today. In particular he created parks and palaces in Surrey.

It became popular to show allegiance by displaying his royal arms in churches. It is regularly stated that this became statutory. Current research has failed to find any such legislation.

The example illustrated is a less common example for being in stained glass. It can be found in a south aisle window of Worplesdon Church.

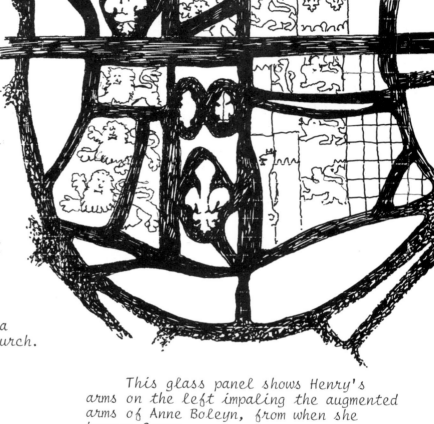

Not all the changes were serious. Medieval gardens absorbed more and more of the Classical ideas being introduced from the Italian renaissance. Topiary was one such idea. Now many Surrey cottage gardens sport such clipped evergreen creations. At Egham, the Elizabethan mansion of Great Fosters Hotel has a fine formal garden with topiary.

This glass panel shows Henry's arms on the left impaling the augmented arms of Anne Boleyn, from when she became Queen.

Anne's have now deteriorated and are even more confusing here without colour.

They are quarterly of six :

1) Lancaster
2) Angouleme
3) Guienne
4) Butler quartering Rockford
5) Brotherton
6) Warenne

Memories of their marriage are evoked again at Great Fosters where her falcon badge is part of a ceiling decoration for reasons now unknown. The former house is said to have been used by Henry as a hunting lodge, it being on the edge of Windsor Great Park. It is also one of the properties to develop from the Dissolution of the Monasteries, it formerly being part of the estates of Chertsey Abbey.

Henry VIII features prominently in the area around Walton-on-Thames where he acquired manor after manor to create vast hunting lands for Hampton Court Palace. Within this 'Honour' he built two more palaces, Nonsuch at Cuddington and Oatlands at Weybridge. Both have been destroyed.

In Loseley House near Guildford can be seen panelling from Nonsuch bearing his and Queen Katherine Parr's initials. Other items from Nonsuch are also present.

Items from Oatlands form part of the display concerning the palace, in Weybridge Museum. Included are the pots sketched below, which came from the palace garderobe.

It was in November 1540, at the Palace of Oatlands, that Henry was secretly married to Catherine Howard in the royal chapel. She was his fifth wife and niece of the Duke of Norfolk who occurs elsewhere in Surrey's history. She was seventeen and beheaded fifteen months later on charges of immorality.

This cheerful little man is Thomas Jonys. At least, it is how the Tudor craftsman imagined him when it came to making his memorial brass for Witley Church.

It was Thomas' job to save King Henry's life. He was "sewer of the chamber". That is not sewer as in needlework but the sewer that is connected with drains. His job was to sample all of the king's food to ensure that it was fit for consumption. He was paid to be poisoned first.

Some books claim that Thomas was not a sewer but a "server". Below is the crucial word, copied from the brass inscription, which certainly seems to be sewer, especially when the letter forms are compared with those in other words on the same inscription.

Celberz

(S e W e r)

The above sketch is a fragment of the view between the Wey Navigation and Old Woking. There is nothing there but a vast open space - great expanses of grassland - The Broadmead. It's just the place to remember Henry VIII.

The Broadmead was adjacent to the old medieval manor house, altered several times, and once the home of Henry's granny, Lady Margaret Beaufort. When, in due course, it became Henry's, he spent much money renovating it into "Woking House". Upon the Broadmead he sported. We are familiar with the colour and extravagance of the tournaments through the modern film recreations. They have been so popular that we can probably picture the Courts of the Tudor more clearly than any other Royal House.

We ponder, perhaps, whether these films give us a very accurate picture of their subject. Evidently one foreign ambassador arrived to find Henry out hawking. King and courtiers were equally resplendent to his foreign eyes and he knew not which was His Majesty.

Here too came many of the other great people of Henry's Court. Thomas Wolsey, Archbishop of York, was high in favour and not just with his king. Here he received a letter from the Pope announcing his election to Cardinal. Sir Thomas More succeeded Wolsey as Lord Chancellor and attended upon the king. So did Thomas Cromwell, who had come to Court as a commoner serving Wolsey. His magnificent success story unfortunately led to his execution but not before he had masterminded the Dissolution of the Monasteries and created revolutionary reforms in administration. Also executed was Sir Francis Weston from nearby Sutton Place, for alleged adultery with Anne Boleyn. Henry's three Queen Catherines came here too.

After the death of Henry VIII the Palace of Woking fell from Royal favour and was allowed to decay. In the reign of James I the king's favourite, Sir Edward Zouch was granted the Woking estates and he eventually persuaded the king to part with them in his favour. The old house provided building materials for his new Hoe Place on the hill above the meadows.

SCHOLA REGIA GRAMMATICALIS
EDVARDI SEXTI 1552

Over the door of the Royal Grammar
School at Guildford are the Royal
Arms as used in the time of Edward VI.
Note the Welsh dragon as supporter
which was to be replaced with a unicorn.
Below the Arms is the inscription shown on
the previous page. These have misled many
people into thinking that the school was started by Edward in 1552.

In fact the first school came into being with a bequest made by a
London grocer named Robert Beckingham. That was in 1509 but it took
another eleven years for the Mayor and Approved Men to get round to
doing anything about it. Their first school was near the castle. It
wasn't a great success so Edward VI was petitioned for a Charter and
regular income with which to start again. Royal Approval was given on
January 27th 1552.

This was a fashionable way of spending money from the Dissolved
Monasteries and thereby trying to show the Reformation in a good light,
not just the whim and greed of the Crown. Even with this beginning the
new school, on the present site, took thirty years to complete.

EDWARD VI   (1537) 1547 - 1553

Despite all the changes in education it still survives today, with
new buildings opposite (entrance sketched above) and has a high reputation.
Among its 'old boys' it claims several bishops but these tend to be over-
shadowed by one Archbishop of Canterbury. He was George Abbot and is best
remembered for another great building in the High Street, the Hospital of
the Blessed Trinity, generally referred to as Abbot's Hospital.

Edward VI was a sickly child much to the consternation of many Protestants who feared his successor would be his Catholic half-sister, Mary Tudor.

When Edward died on 6th July the Protestant succession was invested in his first cousin, Lady Jane Grey. This could not be publicly proclaimed until the country was at its defences against a Catholic rebellion.

LADY JANE GREY

(1537)

1553

London and Surrey were for Jane. One of Surrey's officials was Sir Thomas Cawarden, pronounced Carden. It was as 'Mr. Carden' that he was addressed with 'Mr. Saunders' (Sir Thomas Saunders, Sheriff) in a letter of 8th July, perhaps indicating a hasty despatch.

From the Lords of the Council, it ordered military readiness for the defence of the County and the unusual instruction to support all previous ordinances. These normally died with the monarch, to be re-established by the successor but Jane was not to be publicly proclaimed until the next day.

The Surrey officials received a letter from Jane dated 11th July in which she reminded them of their duty to ensure her succession. Shrewdly, this opportunity was taken to confirm the Lieutenant's appointment and to promise its renewal.

On 16th July she wrote again to remind all Surrey gentry of their allegiance to her. The same day the Lords in Council wrote too. They were alarmed by all the gossip which they tried to counter with a reminder of what Mary's Catholicism would mean to them all as Protestants. They asserted that it was not treasonable to support Jane because Jane was queen, even if not yet officially so.

Their own allegiance was short-lived. On 19th July they wrote again, including the Earl of Surrey, to proclaim a new Queen.....Mary Tudor. Jane wrote that day too. She demanded tents for the troops but unbeknown to her these had now gone over to Mary's cause.

That day too another letter was sent to Sir Thomas Cawarden. This one came from the Gentlemen of Kent, proclaiming that Mary was queen. One of the signatories was 'T.Wyatt', presumed to be Sir Thomas Wyatt of the forthcoming 'Wyatt's Rebellion'.

Finally that day, Jane entered the Tower, not as queen to await her coronation ceremony but as a prisoner. She was executed the following February, still only sixteen years old.

National rejoicing brought Mary to the throne.

Most of these comings and goings occured at the house of the chief agent for Surrey, Sir William More, at Loseley, near Guildford. His emblem was the moorhen (illustrated) which can be seen paddling around the moat of the old house. The present house was built shortly afterwards (1562-1568) by the same Sir William More.

Part of ruins of Woking Palace.

MARY I   1516 (1553 – 1558)

It is said, locally, that after studying dates on documents a claim has been made that Mary Tudor could not have been born at Greenwich as is usually stated. Instead her birthplace was the royal palace at Woking. The palace is now (1984) severely ruined but the press report negotiations towards preserving it as a monument. At present it is on private property without public access.

In July 1554 Mary arrived at the Bishop's Palace, Farnham to stay with her trusted advisor, Bishop Gardiner. It was she who released him from prison upon the death of Edward VI and he who crowned her in Westminster Abbey. Now they were to travel on to Winchester Cathedral where he would marry her to Philip II of Spain. Their attempts to reconcile England with the Church of Rome would label her "Bloody Mary" and him "Hammer of the Heretics" for their execution of so many Protestants. None of these came from Surrey.

The Catholic marriage provoked "Wyatt's Rebellion" and the attempt to put Protestant Elizabeth on the throne. The Kentish leaders had already written to Surrey's Sir Thomas Cawarden and so had Mary. On January 25th 1554 she instructed him to arm his servants and guard his neighbourhood. That day, however, he was arrested and was taken before the Council but was discharged. Obviously he was under great suspicion.

On 26th January the rebellion broke out in Kent while Mary was instructing Sheriff Saunders to obey Admiral Lord William Howard whom she had commissioned to control Kent and Surrey. He certainly didn't* Cawarden and must have had some 'intelligence' because on the 27th he rearrested Cawarden and put him in the Clink. He sent Saunders to Cawarden's at Blechingley and there they found an astonishing arsenal. On the 28th Howard ordered Saunders to seize the arsenal. It was sufficient to arm 110 mounted and over 300 fighters on foot. Why it should have been amassed is not clear as the rebellion had not been long in the plotting.

Cawarden was now under house arrest at his home at Blackfriars. Nothing could be proved against him and so he had to be released. That must have been with great misgivings. The arms were prudently kept.

* trust

The little village of Chobham must have been an
unlikely place to find the former Archbishop of York
and yet Mary sold him the manor for £3,000. He was
Nicholas Heath who is now buried in the church
(plain blue marble slab in the chancel floor).
    As Bishop of Worcester he refused to take the
oath for Henry VIII's Act of Supremacy and
refused later reforms too. He went to the Tower.
Mary reinstated him; John Hooper having been
holding his see in the meantime, but Mary had
him burnt, at Gloucester.
    Nicholas Heath rose to be Archbishop
and then Lord Chancellor and later
proclaimed Elizabeth queen. She
visited him in his retirement at
Chobham.

    The name Marsh Marigold does not come from Mary's Gold as is
so often claimed. Thus its association with Queen Mary and before
that with the Blessed Virgin Mary is false. It is a corruption
of its Saxon name, 'merisc' for marsh, plus gold.

53.

ELIZABETH I
(1533)
1588 ~ 1603

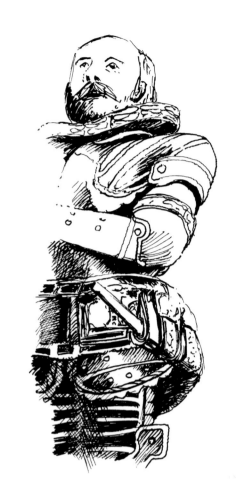

With this reign it is probably Sir Francis Drake and the Spanish Armada that come to mind first. They may seem far from Surrey but not a bit of it.

Sir Francis wrote from his ship to Walsingham, the Queen's secretary, about presenting her with his prisoners, including Don Pedro de Valdez: "Their Don Pedro is a man of great estimation with the King of Spain, and thought next in his army to the Duke of Sidonia".

Don Pedro and Co. were handed over to Drake's relative, Sir Richard Drake, for protective custody at Esher. Sir Richard kneels (right) on his monument in Christ Church, Esher. He had been to the East Indies with Sir Francis and was an equerry of Elizabeth's stables.

Preparations for the Armada were less successful in Surrey. Lord High Admiral Howard of Effingham couldn't get the men he wanted and had to accept bowmen. By July 28th he'd raised 1,871 of which 836 were stationed at Dorking.

Perhaps Sir Richard Drake got involved, as equerry, with another Surrey problem. There weren't enough horses. This was no new problem. An Act for increasing horses was made by Henry VII. His successor still had a problem. It took over a hundred horses to move his Court and so extra were regularly brought in from Middlesex. Elizabeth complained to Surrey. Anyone with a park over one mile in circumference had to keep brood mares. Thirty six of these parks were to be shown by Speed on his ever popular map of the County. Elizabeth was the first monarch to cross the County from north to south since the reign of Edward I. The enormous convoy must have been most impressive. "Elizabeth slept here" is true for such places as Loseley.

She came here in 1576, 1583 and 1591. Her needlework can be seen on the cushions of two Elizabethan Maid of Honour chairs in the drawing room, which are thought to be her handiwork. The present house was new then, having been built by her host, and special favourite, William More, whom she knighted in 1576. He was her chief and most trusted agent for the administration of Surrey.

Newt Haw
1978

Ottershaw
1975.

Christ was the worde and spake it
He took the bread and break it,
And what the worde doth make it,
That I believe and take it.

In the parish church of Walton-on-Thames visitors are confronted with two very different insights into the reign of Elizabeth. One is the verse printed here which can be found upon the pillar by the pulpit. It is reputed to have been put there by Elizabeth as a testament to her faith at Holy Communion.

The other is this extraordinary scene from the memorial to John Selwyn on the north wall. The inscribed brass illustrates an incident that is said to have taken place in nearby Oatlands Park. Selwyn was her game keeper there and on a hunting expedition he is said to have leapt upon the back of a charging stag and by stabbing it through the throat brought it down at the Queen's feet.

Thursley 1976

55.

LOSELEY - Walking across the lawns from the car park, this is the impressive frontage that visitors face. The building stones came from Waverley Abbey. Once there was a side wing on the end nearest the viewer but even without it the building generates a sense of anticipation which the interior doesn't disappoint. Some rare material brought from Nonsuch Palace takes us back to Henry VIII and that king's Great Collar can be seen in the portrait of Edward VI. Nearby is William IV's coronation chair and from recent times, a photograph of Queen Mary on her visit in 1932. The library fireplace carving bears the arms of Elizabeth I and the date 1570. In her footsteps we tread the stairs to her bedroom with its original bed. Even the curtains are original.

The adjoining bedroom was used by James I who stayed twice at Loseley. Thus the carpet shows not only the crown and the Tudor rose but also the thistle of Scotland. To commemorate his visits the king presented full length portraits by the court painter of himself and his queen, Anne of Denmark. These portraits now hang in the Great Hall. In the nearby drawing room we can see the ceiling that was redecorated specially for one of those visits. By this time the Master of the House was no longer Sir William but his son, Sir George More, whom King James made Chancellor of the Order of the Garter. He was also Treasurer to the king's son, Prince Henry.

JAMES I
(1566)
1603 ~ 1625

James I may have had
weak legs but he was
fine on horseback and
a keen huntsman. This
was bad news for the
people of Surrey who
were still trying to
rid themselves of the
remains of Forest Law.

The districts around all
the royal parks had to
be cleared of pigs in
case they rutted the
woodland rides and
unseated the king when
galloping at speed.

In 1603 he visited Farnham
Castle and noted the good hunting
thereabouts. In 1608 he leased
the castle and park from the Bishop of
Winchester for the rest of Bishop Bilson's lifetime. However, it was only the next
year that he leased it out to Ramsay, Viscount Haddington, as a reward for his
services during the Gowrie Plot. Nevertheless, the king remained a frequent visitor
which was just as well for the estate cost him a lot of money. It had fallen on hard
times and attempts to re-fence it were thwarted when his neighbours took the fencing
for firewood. Some even moved in as squatters. The sketch shows part of the
medieval castle from the park. The public has access to both.

James's hunting exploits gave rise to numerous tales. It is said that after
a successful kill he daubed his courtiers with blood. It is also said that when
the deer's entrails were removed he bathed his legs in the beast's stomach to cure
his gout etc. Such exploits could have done little to overcome the local prejudice
against the barbarian Scots. It wouldn't overcome gout either!

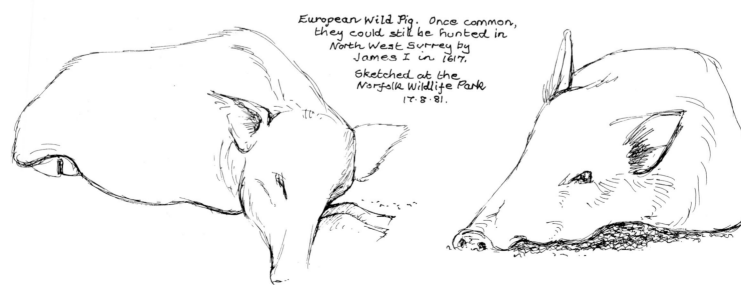

European Wild Pig. Once common,
they could still be hunted in
North West Surrey by
James I in 1617.

Sketched at the
Norfolk Wildlife Park
17.8.81.

From this reign and from these hunting expeditions comes another story of national interest. In March 1605 London heard that the king had been murdered at Woking. What food for gossip that was! Had he been shot or had he been stabbed? Perhaps he'd been poisoned? Who had done it - one of the embittered English or Scottish factions or some evil foreign agent?

The House of Lords despatched an investigator. Upon his arrival at Woking he found the king in fine spirits boosting his health with outdoor activities - hunting. This he curtailed to return to London to "show himself" to his people. The panic was over. The crowds went home.

Scots Pine
Virginia Water
20.3.76

There are many stories about James at Woking with his host and favourite, Sir Edward Zouch. Not only did Zouch bring in extra deer to the park to please his king but trees too. James was familiar with the Scots Pine from his homeland but in southern England it had been extinct for centuries. Zouch, however, got some seedlings from a relative. The tree became fashionable and nowadays it has naturalised itself all over the Surrey Commons. The Forestry Commission Survey of 1979-82 records 3785 ha of Scots Pine in Surrey. It's the commonest conifer and third commonest tree after oak and birch.

Other places have connections with James. To Oatlands at Weybridge he came with his queen prior to his coronation and he was subsequently to grant her the property. His Keeper of the Park has a brass in Weybridge church. James and Anne were the last royal owners of Byfleet Manor and their arms appear in stained glass in Abbot's Hospital at Guildford.* The castle there was sold into private ownership by James. At Wanborough James knighted his host but Sir Walter Raleigh he had executed. His wife and his head are buried at West Horsley.

At this time there were changes in Surrey's industries too, from silk and paper to glass. A royal proclamation from 1615 forbade the use of timber as fuel. This had dire consequences on those industries with wood fuelled furnaces such as glass manufacture. So, after hundreds of years, it lost its pre-eminence and died out. Centres in more northern parts of the country, with easy access to coal, took over.

* window not in parts shown to visitors.

59.

B. Howkins
1984
Canal Scene
West Surrey.

CHARLES I
(1600)
1625 ~ 1649

This is the monarch that gave royal approval to a scheme that has created a major landscape feature of West Surrey; the Wey Navigation.

It was the idea of Sir Richard Weston of Sutton Place near Guildford. From travelling in Europe as a young man, especially in the Low Countries, he returned with ideas that would eventually develop into a scheme for making the River Wey navigable from Guildford down to Weybridge and the Thames. Thus a new trade route would be opened to London and its docks. This was the first (debatable) major scheme of its type in England and so funds were rather slow to amass. Royal approval was sought to boost this and so it should have done. Unfortunately for Sir Richard it was 1635 before he was made one of the royal commissioners to explore the idea fully. The country was becoming increasingly disillusioned with the king and this was no time to be dubbed a royalist. To make matters worse Sir Richard was known to be a Roman Catholic recusant. In 1642 Civil War broke and Richard had to flee to Holland. His estates were seized by Parliament.

Sir Richard was a determined man and through the agency of friendly parliamentarians he was able to retrieve much of his former status. The project went ahead with astonishing speed but King Charles was executed before its completion in 1653 and Sir Richard himself died just a few months too soon.

The Wey Navigation and its extension to Godalming (1760) are explored more fully in Chris. Howkins' "Towpath Book" in this series.

It's a beautiful walk along the footpaths through woods and fields to the ponds at Imbhams. It is now difficult to visualise this landscape near Chiddingfold as once being the centre of heavy industry. Nevertheless, the water once powered the hammers of the Quenell's ironworks here.

Peter Quenell (1580-1650) was making guns for Charles I at the beginning of the Civil War. Surrey was for Parliament (except the Farnham area) and so inevitably Parliament decided that they must stop this supply to the king.

Quenell's son, another Peter, who worked in the family business, decided to resist any such attempt. This was not just out of loyalty to the king but because guns had been supplied on credit and they would soon be out of business if debts were not recovered soon. In 1642 a royalist band of seventy two defended the site but only twenty four were fully armed and five were not armed at all. The County Authorities soon overpowered them. They also took control of the gunpowder mills at Chilworth.

Imbhams 1984.
Pond.

The splendid timbered house of the Quenell ironmasters is now Lythe Hill Hotel at Haslemere. More details of this family's history can be found in the records of Compton near Guildford where they had Field Place. Beware, at least five were called Peter !

In 1648 when Charles was taken from Hurst Castle to his execution at Whitehall he passed through the garrison town of Farnham. There on 20th December he spent the night in Vernon House. For this occasion he was put in the safe custody of a General Harrison who, despite being an enemy, made a favourable impression on Charles.

Vernon House, in West Street, is now used by Surrey County Library.

CHARLES II
(1630) 1660-1685

It's time a royal mistress appeared in these pages! Charles II had at least nine whose children were acknowledged as his. One of these ladies lived briefly in the "Old Manor House" in the main street of Old Woking. She was Barabara Villiers, alias Mrs Roger Palmer, later Countess of Castlemaine and then Duchess of Cleveland. Through her, Charles fathered Anne, Countess of Sussex, Charles Fitzroy, Duke of Southampton, Henry Fitzroy, Duke of Grafton, Charlotte, Countess of Lichfield and George Fitzroy, Duke of Northumberland.

The house (illustrated) was built in 1622 by Sir Edward Zouch, a royal favourite since James I. His son, a Royalist Captain was killed in the Civil War without leaving an heir so the house reverted to the Crown. In 1671 Charles granted it to Barbara. In 1708 she moved in personally but died the following year. Her children sold the property out of the family and so the royal visits for hunting in Woking Park came to an end. So did the entertainments for the ladies which in recent years had raised an eyebrow or two. The former palace had been pulled down by this time and the materials used elsewhere, in this house and in a grander house on top of the hill overlooking the Wey Valley. This was to be Hoe Place of which part survives among the more recent buildings. Another reminder of Zouch is the West Gallery of 1622 in the church.

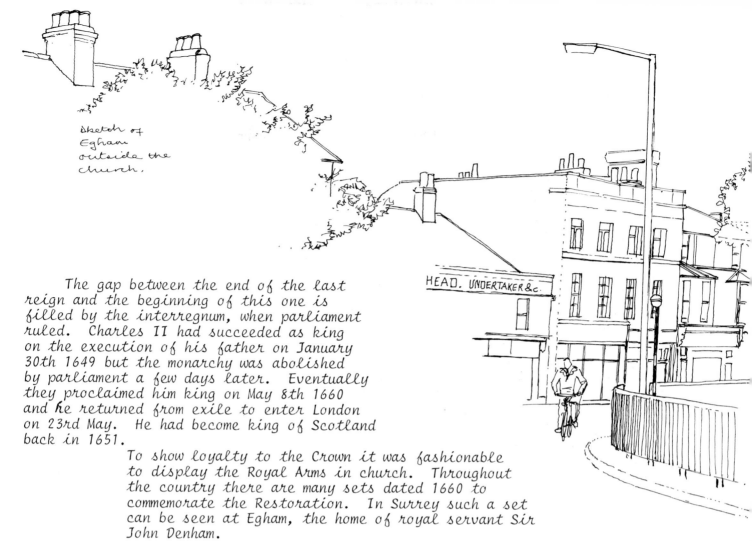

Sketch of
Egham
outside the
church.

HEAD. UNDERTAKER &c.

The gap between the end of the last
reign and the beginning of this one is
filled by the interregnum, when parliament
ruled. Charles II had succeeded as king
on the execution of his father on January
30th 1649 but the monarchy was abolished
by parliament a few days later. Eventually
they proclaimed him king on May 8th 1660
and he returned from exile to enter London
on 23rd May. He had become king of Scotland
back in 1651.

To show loyalty to the Crown it was fashionable
to display the Royal Arms in church. Throughout
the country there are many sets dated 1660 to
commemorate the Restoration. In Surrey such a set
can be seen at Egham, the home of royal servant Sir
John Denham.

It is regularly stated, the present writer included, that
the Royal Arms were introduced by law under Henry VIII
and that the law still prevails. Recent searches have
failed to produce that law or any convincing reference to it.

Weybridge

Royal visits also served to promote other new ventures. Back in the 1750's
the people of Weybridge were able to enjoy locally grown pineapples. From the
century before that came the painting by Henry Danckerts showing Charles II
receiving the first pineapple grown in England, at Dorney House, near Weybridge.
It was being offered by the Royal Gardener. His name was Rose! It is now
thought that the inscription is in error, that the Dorney House refers to one
in Buckinghamshire and not the one at Weybridge where Henry VIII was nursed as a
baby. That house has now been demolished and modern housing covers the site.

JAMES II

(1633)

1685~1689

It is not difficult to imagine this doorway as the entrance to a prison, especially on a cold winter's day when the shadow of the opposite building falls across it. However, the Hospital of the Blessed Trinity was built for a totally different purpose. Known affectionately as "Abbot's Hospital" it was founded in 1619 by Guildford's famous son, George Abbot, who became Archbishop of Canterbury. His birthplace has been demolished but the school he attended is nearby (see Edward VI) and his tomb is in Holy Trinity Church opposite the Hospital. That was founded as an Old People's Home for the elderly of Guildford and it still serves that purpose. Visitors are shown parts of it, with its royal connections with the first King James, its superb collection of contemporary furnishings and its architecture of national importance.

For just one night it became a prison. The prisoner was James, an illegitimate but staunchly Protestant son of Charles II by his mistress Lucy Walters. He became the Duke of Monmouth who led the Protestant rebellion against the Catholicism of James II. It was Monmouth's illegitimacy that precluded him from being heir to the throne and Charles refused to legitimise him despite the rumours of 1662. After the "Rye House Plot" to kill Charles he was exiled and had to await the natural death of his father. Then he moved to fulfil his ambitions. Back from Belgium he came to lead the Monmouth rebellion, culminating in his defeat at the Battle of Sedgemoor near Bridgwater, Somerset on July 6th 1685. It had been feared that troops might have reached a position much nearer to London and so the new King sent his own to West Surrey and Farnham became a garrison town.

Monmouth was captured miles away, in a Dorset*ditch, but nevertheless came through Surrey to spend his last night alive in Guildford. Since then the High Street has been cobbled and paved but he would still recognise Abbot's Hospital. No doubt he was already familiar with 'Dutch gables' from his continental exile. The Royal Arms of the first King James, now over the doorway, were not put up until 1825. Inside, the muniment room-cum-treasury was used for his custody and is still preserved as the "Monmouth Room" but is not normally shown to visitors.

From Guildford, Monmouth went the next day to face his king, his death sentence and his execution on Tower Hill. It was July 15th 1685.

The Monmouth Rebellion had a more important effect upon Guildford. With its threat to the country south of the capital, James needed assurance of its loyalty but Guildford, so strategically placed, was in decline and had even had its ancient Charter confiscated. This was now promptly re-issued and in its original form too. From later comes a story of the Corporation getting a good fright when they found themselves involved in a treason charge. They had been given a chain and medal of office by Onslow of Clandon Park and this showed the king's arms on one side and Onslow's on the other. That was just what the royal authorities were looking for to get at Onslow who had successfully dared to block the workings of one of Judge "Bloody" Jeffries' courts at Guildford. The defendents, on charges of poaching the king's deer, had turned to the great Onslow family for support and got it. A subsequent speech by Onslow was also inflamatory. Then came the medal and Onslow's prosecution. He was not executed for treason but bound over to keep the peace.

* Hampshire by some accounts.

WILLIAM III
(1650) 1689 - 1702

MARY (1662) 1689 - 1694

Until her death in 1694
Mary II and William III reigned
jointly by Act of Parliament -
a new development in the English
notion of kingship.

When William landed at Tor Bay
on November 5th 1688 and James II
rushed to his army, a battle was
expected in West Surrey.
This frightened
a notable statesman and diplomat into
fleeing his new house at Moor Park, Farnham,
believing it would be the site of the
battle. There was no battle. James fled.

The statesman was Sir William Temple
and several times he was visited at Moor Park
by his new sovereign, William III.

Both would have difficulty
recognising the place today.
The entrance logia remains
much the same with
Temple's arms above.
These are of cast iron
which was an important
industry in West Surrey.
Many fire-backs have
survived which date
from this time.
The arms would
remind the Dutch king
that his new English
subjects had power and
tradition to be respected.
At first he knew little
English but could evidently
reassure us with "I will
maintain, I will maintain".

Temple was soon laying out his new garden in the fashionable 'Dutch' style,
complete with canal. No doubt the king appreciated this on his visits. The Dutch
were not the originators of this style but had taken much of it from France.
Among Temple's writings was "An Essay on Gardening" and before buying Moor Park
he had some of the earliest greenhouses at his London home (now The Old Deer Park,
Richmond). Alas the garden at Moor Park has now been too greatly modified to
show us Temple's ideas. It, nor the house, were open to the public at the time
of writing - 1984.

Opposite sketch: a great Magnolia in the walled garden of Moor Park.
Magnolias had not been introduced in Temple's time.

During these visits William III met
Jonathan Swift, who was the tutor of Esther
Johnson, whose mother was companion to Temple's
sister. There is a popular story that here King William
taught Swift to pick asparagus the Dutch way; also that the
king offered him a troop of horse. In contrast, it is also
said that the king disliked Swift and refused him preferment in the
church. Relations were sufficiently good at one time for Swift to be
sent, unsuccessfully, to persuade the king to renew parliament every
three years. One of the king's great partisans was Sir Richard Onslow who
began rebuilding the present Clandon Park. He was Knight of the Shire in
the Convention Parliament that passed the crown to William and Mary.

At Moor Park, Temple's young secretary, Jonathan Swift, wrote "The
Battle of the Books" and "The Tale of the Tub". Gulliver came later.
Here too he fell in love with Esther who was the 'Stella' of the journal
he wrote to her. She was eight; he was twenty two.

Queen Mary's treasurer was Sir
Edward Nicholas of West Horsley Place
and patron of the church. Tradition
says that King William presented the
church with a brass candelabrum.

Forest Law was finally lifted in
1694 when William put in writing that
Surrey was "now out of the Forest".
The Forest Law had lasted for over
600 years.

William continued the royal patronage
of horse racing which had been popularised
by Charles II. To the Guildford Races, held
at Merrow, William gave the King's Plate of 100 guineas.

ANNE (1665) 1702~1714

Chertsey keeps alive the tradition
that Queen Anne came there but no one
seems to have been able to substantiate
this. Another problem is why the old house
behind the Georgian facade, in Windsor Street,
is called Denmark House. The two may be connected.
If it was the wrong Anne then the story may arise from
Anne of Denmark, Queen to James I. She could well have
come by river to Chertsey en route for her manor house at
Byfleet which she had rebuilt. This would then be a case of updating.

Many historical stories were updated to keep them topical.
At nearby Addlestone survives the Crouch Oak, a boundary tree of Windsor
Great Park. Some people say Elizabeth I had a picnic under it. Others
will assert that it was Queen Victoria. It depends who's fashionable or
topical.

In the illustration above, the building to the left of Denmark House is
the Swan. Here Victoria stopped, stabled her horses but didn't sleep.
She spent the night next door, in Denmark House.

Queen Anne didn't play a very active role in the districts
under consideration in this book. At Weybridge, however, she
was patron of the church and five incumbents served during that
period. The church they knew became too cramped and humble for
Victorian Weybridge, rapidly expanding in the railway age and so
it was rebuilt in 1848 by J.L.Pearson, who did quite a lot of
work in Surrey. An extra aisle had to be added sixteen years
later. It is his church that we see today.

GEORGE I
(1660)
1714 ~ 1727

" But if such things no more encourage
The taste of a politer age,
To help them out in time of need
Another Tofts must rabbits breed. "

C. Churchill, Ghost, i, 435-8.

Ever since the Normans introduced them we have always had room in our affections for rabbits. So when Mary Tofts of Godalming was said to have given birth to live rabbits she was soon common gossip well beyond the County boundary. Society ladies flocked to see her, street singers traded on her and so did the producers of broadsheets, cartoons etc. The King and the Prince of Wales were equally fascinated and set up an investigation which dragged on for months and has left a story that is often retold but which has numerous variations. This is my version but I cannot guarantee it's right.........

Mary Tofts claimed that when she was working in the hop fields on April 23rd 1726 a rabbit reared up and scared her. On Spetember 27th she was taken so seriously ill that her clothier husband sent to Guildford for Mr. Howard, a doctor. It was he who reported the birth of five live rabbits. By November 9th when he wrote to a Mr Davenant on the matter he was able to report that further births had occurred to a total of twelve. Good old Mary !

The news had reached the Palace and the Prince of Wales despatched his secretary with the royal anatomist and surgeon, Mr. Nathaniel St. Andre. They arrived at Guildford, to which Mary had been moved for convenience, in time to be present for the birth of the fifteenth rabbit and for a further two. They were satisfied that no fraud was involved.

Producing the first, third, fifth and ninth rabbits as evidence, they were able to convince the king and Drs Steigerthal and Tessier. However, the German king was not to be easily fooled by the English countrywoman so he sent off another royal surgeon, Mr. Cyriacus Ahlers. He triumphantly returned with the sixteenth rabbit. At about the same time St. Andre returned with a Mr. D'Antenay in time for the birth of two more. At this point it is difficult to keep a total but seventeen or eighteen will do. Also about this time the people involved began making sworn statements with witnesses as to the truth of this phenomenom; an action they were to regret. At this stage too, Mr. Howard asked Ahlers about the possibilty of them all getting a royal pension when the fuss was over. Now that's an interesting idea ! Alas, on the scene comes the highly reputable Sir Richard Manningham M.D. F.R.S., sent by the king and with the gravest of suspicions.

Mary laid on a convulsion for him but he was not impressed. He had her removed to Lacy's Bagnio in Leicester Fields - to the delight of the society ladies of London. Dr. Douglas, obstetrician, came too.

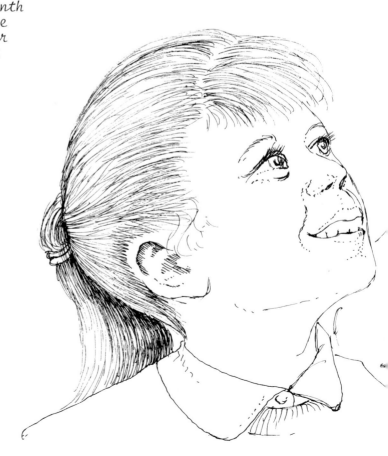

Thomas Howard now enters the story with an interesting story of his own. He introduced himself to Justice of the Peace, Sir Thomas Clarges Bt. and swore that he had obtained a rabbit for Mary. Aha! Mary said it was for food but Clarges knew all about cross-examinations of course and was very good at it. Very soon he had confessions to fraud.

The country loved it! First a good story and now they could laugh their heads off at the doctors who had sworn it was all true.....

Most true it is, I dare to say,
 E're since the days of Eve
The weakest woman sometimes may
 The wisest man deceive.

So ran part of one of the street songs that she inspired. What happened next I haven't been able to trace very clearly.

On January 21st 1764 it was reported in the "Weekly Miscellany" that "the celebrated rabbit woman" was convicted of receiving stolen goods and sent to Guildford gaol. That is also the month in which she is said to have died.

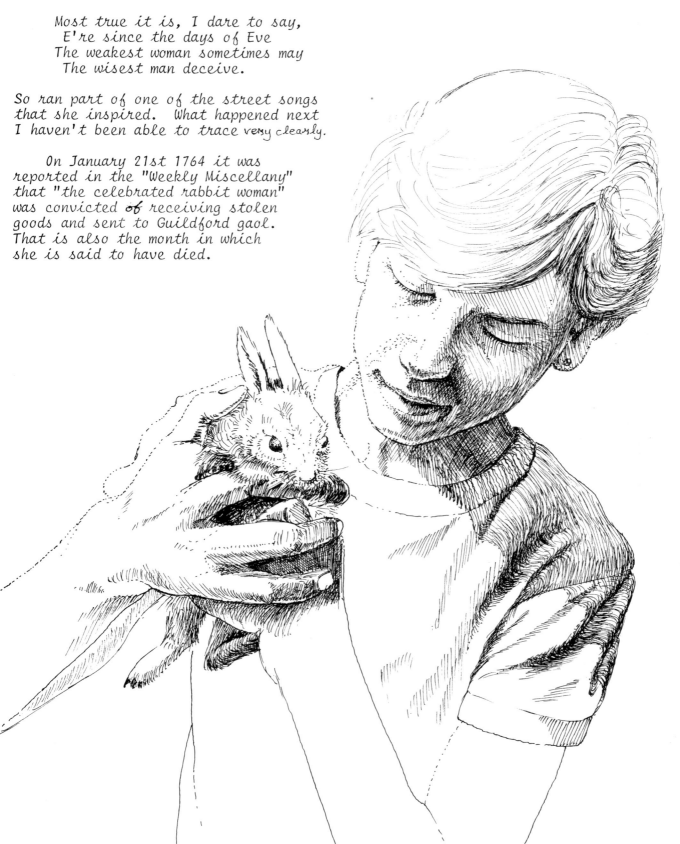

71.

GEORGE II

(1683) 1727 - 1760

Having lost the lands in France centuries ago, the kingdom was now expanding again with fresh colonies. In the New World the southern third of Carolina remained largely unsettled until 1733. In January of that year over 100 colonists with a royal governor arrived at what is now Savannah. With their royal charter they founded a new colony, named in honour of the king - GEORGIA.

The king chose his governor from Surrey, one James Edward Oglethorpe. He lived at Westbrook House in Godalming. That house, in Westbrook Lane, still stands but has been embellished since Oglethorpe's day. A portion is illustrated above.

A more obvious link can be seen in Haslemere High Street where the Georgian Hotel commemorates the new colony. This building was the town house of Oglethorpe when he was staying at Haslemere as their Member of Parliament.

Haslemere received Borough status in 1584 but was disfranchised as a 'rotten' borough by the 1832 Reform Bill and ceased to be a borough after the Municipal Reform Act of 1835. It was between 1722-54 that Oglethorpe served five times as Member of Parliament.

As a great philanthropist he served to better the lot of the poor. By the end of the 18thC. 13½% of the population was in receipt of Poor Relief. Surrey was badly affected but this was no new problem. Back in the reign of Elizabeth I action was sought to combat vagabonds on Surrey's roads. This situation largely arose from Henry VIII's Dissolution of the Monasteries. The monastic lands of Chertsey and Waverley Abbeys, Newark Priory etc. covered much of West Surrey, providing food, employment, lodgings and other relief. Oglethorpe's new colony was for debtors. He envisaged a landscape of small farms and so the Charter forbade the importation of coloured people. This was to prevent slavery and the development of plantations. That law changed by 1750. Oglethorpe was no longer Governor. After nine good years he was forced to return to England in 1743. He was heavily in debt himself, having lent his money to his colonists.

His complete biography is full of interest and as far as Surrey is concerned involves interests in land at Bramley, Compton, Elstead, Puttenham and Tongham. He eventually settled at Cranham, Essex, now part of Greater London.

The changing role of kingship is highlighted by an incident in parliament when Colonel Fitzroy was late because he had been waiting on the king. "Sir, don't tell me of waiting; this is your place to attend in - this is your first duty," retorted the Speaker. That Speaker was Arthur Onslow. He saw in the new reign and saw out five parliaments; he saw the fall of Walpole, the first Prime Minister and he saw the rise of Pitt the Elder.

Several generations of Onslows served Surrey and parliament and have left their impress on much of our history. From Arthur we derive much of the parliamentary procedure in use today and the full keeping of parliamentary records.

Today the Onslows are associated with Clandon Park (National Trust) but Arthur did not live in this house even though his library and collection of portraits are now there. His home was Imber (Ember) Court, Thames Ditton (now Metropolitan Police Mounted Training Establishment). He was buried (1768) at Thames Ditton but later moved to Merrow.

His king was our last to lead troops into battle and Arthur himself was threatened with violence at Guildford during the riots that broke out at the beginning of the Seven Years War. The Surrey leader was a farmer called Worsfold. Arthur Onslow had been made Recorder for Guildford in 1737. He also served the Rotten Borough of Haslemere. Of more note, he was made Chancellor to Queen Caroline in 1729.

Clandon Park was largely complete by 1729 and the great marble Hall is hailed as one of the finest Palladian examples in the country — the great house of a great family.

b. Howkins
1983
Mole Valley
Mickleham

GEORGE III (1738) 1760~1820

Much of West Surrey is still agricultural so it's a natural subject to recall when thinking of George III. Not only did he coincide with much of the Agrarian Revolution but took a personal interest in the matter, hence his nickname, "Farmer George". The influence of Surrey continues outwards into the developing Empire. Just as George II took us to the American Colonies so George III takes us to those in South Africa.

The story can be found in St. George's churchyard, Esher. Here, at the east end, can be found a table tomb inscribed:

IN MEMORY OF MR WILLIAM DUCKITT
SON OF THE ABOVE MR WILLIAM AND MRS ELIZABETH DUCKITT WHO DEPARTED THIS LIFE IN THE 53RD YEAR OF HIS AGE AT THE CAPE OF GOOD HOPE ON THE 13TH APRIL 1825 TO WHICH SETTLEMENT HE WAS SENT WITH A LARGE ESTABLISHMENT BY HIS MAJESTY GEO 3RD TO INTRODUCE HIS FATHER'S SYSTEM AND IMPLEMENTS OF AGRICULTURE INTO THAT COLONY IN THE YEAR 1800.

Changes in agriculture continue. This hay-
making scene in the Mole Valley at Mickleham is
rapidly becoming a thing of the past as silage
proves more reliable. Wheat has given way to
Barley as the County's chief cereal crop and
that is changing too with higher yields from
winter barley than the more traditional spring
barley.

This landscape was familiar to another
character from the stories of the royal court
at this time - Fanny Burney, the novelist.

She had served as Second Keeper of the
Robes to Queen Charlotte but the job didn't
suit her in the least. She had accepted the
offer to please her father as much as anything.
Her health worn down, she left Court and went to
stay with her sister at Mickleham. Just up the
road were living some French refugees whom she
met and socialised with, causing concern for her
reputation. Nevertheless she fell in love with
one General Alexandre D'Arblay who had been
Adjutant General to Lafayette and thus an enemy
of the State in some people's eyes. They were
married in Mickleham church. They also loved
the district and its people, both of which can
be detected in her writings.

She began writing
her novel "Camilla" in a house now gone but
commemorated in the hamlet of Camilla Lacey.
Then they moved over the hill to Great Bookham
to the red brick house that still stands boldly
in the High Street. In February 1796 she
received a letter from Court granting permission
to dedicate "Camilla" to the Queen. This was
a surprising gesture to one who had so recently
caused offence, especially bearing in mind
that the Queen was no enthusiast of novels or
novelists and certainly not female novelists.

In July Fanny and Alexander set off for
Windsor with two sets of "Camilla" to present
to the royal family (the novel was published
in five volumes). The reconciliation was a
great success - quite moving, with twists of
the unexpected and not without humour. It is
best read in the personal writings of Fanny
Burney which have been published. You won't
find 18thC. stuffiness there!

The subscription list for "Camilla"
includes Jane Austen, then aged eighteen.
Her Godfather was the incumbent of Great
Bookham. She too was to use the local
scenes in her own novels. Is it coincidence
that 'pride and prejudice' is printed three
times in block capitals in the final
paragraph of Fanny Burney's "Camilla".

Duckitt, the father, as an
inventor of agricultural machinery
and a pioneer of new practices,
became a friend of George III.
He was visited by the king at
his home, Waylands Farm, Hersham.
He also rented Sandown Farm at
Esher. They probably talked
gardening too. George was
devoted to his garden, now part
of the Royal Botanic Gardens,
Kew, while William, when younger,
had worked in the gardens of the
Duke of Newcastle at Claremont,
Esher (recently restored by the
National Trust).

N.B. Duckitt is spelt with
an 'i' on the tomb but with an
'e' in many books.

GEORGE IV
(1765)
1820 ~
1830

By the lake at Virginia Water, in the Surrey part of Windsor Great Park are Roman ruins. They were brought from Lepcis Magna near Tripoli, in 1816 and given to the Prince Regent for the portico of the British Museum. Instead they were erected here in 1826.

'They turned the church into a tulip bed', complained an Esher resident of the High Society crowds. In all their finery, they flocked to St. George's to be seen in the presence of Princess Charlotte. Heir to the throne and only child of George IV, she was adored by the nation. From 1816 she lived at Claremont, after her marriage to Prince Leopold of Saxe-Coburg, but the affectionate mobbing deterred her from attending church. Soon she resorted to private worship with her chaplain at Claremont. Within a few months the country was delighted to hear that she was with child. Then in November 1817 she died in childbirth. The whole country seemed to mourn.

Leopold became King of the Belgians in 1831. He was nephew to Prince Albert.

St. George's (above) with Christ
Church and Claremont, make Esher the
richest corner of Surrey for royal history of
the late 18th/19th centuries. Nearby at Weybridge
Church is a monument to Frederica, Duchess of York, who
lived at Oatlands. "The Monument" at the foot of Monument
Hill, Weybridge, is also to her.

        Claremont is the earliest surviving landscape
garden (begun before 1720) and has recently been restored by the National
Trust. The house is not open to
the public.

George, as Prince of
Wales, won the Derby
at Epsom with
"Sir Thomas" in
1788. It started
odds on chance.

The sketch below is of the old Town Hall in Haslemere High Street. Originally Haslemere was made a borough by Elizabeth I to strengthen her support in the House of Commons. Now, in this reign, it lost that status, together with Surrey's other "rotten boroughs" of Ble-chingley and Gatton. By this time much royal power had been delegated to parliament but on this issue of the 1832 Reform Act William intervened by threatening to increase the number of peers until the opposition was out-voted. For electoral purposes Surrey was now divided into west and east. The former comprised Godley, Elmbridge, Woking, Effingham, Copthorne, Farnham, Godalming, Blackheath, Wotton, with Guildford as the election town. The electorate was increased by about 50% with new voting rights going mainly to the middle classes.

WILLIAM IV
(1765) 1830~1837

In the year of William's accession there was revolution in France and Belgium and growing unrest in England due to falling wages and a series of bad harvests. There were echoes of the 'Peasants' Revolt' (1381) all over again. The southern counties rose against the employers. Locally, the most hated received letters signed by "Captain Swing" demanding that the use of machinery be discontinued. Their determination was emphasised by arson attacks in November (1830). Firemen at Egham had three in one night to contend with, only to find that their hose had been sabotaged. Corn stacks were popular targets and were soon blazing at Guildford and Capel. The corn mill was the target at Albury and the miller was shot at. This went on for two weeks; long enough to alarm the authorities.

Thus on Monday 22nd November magistrates met at the Red Lion, Dorking (demolished) to swear in special constables. News of this leaked and spread so fast that even before they had finished the main street (right) filled with agricultural workers armed with cudgels. Every window in the Red Lion was smashed and a magistrate stoned unconscious. The armed yeomanry moved in, arresting eleven and reading the Riot Act.

Unlike Richard II, William did not need to face the rioters personally; society was now structured to deal with such events. Instead, he issued a Royal Proclamation against rioters in the Southern Counties and mobilised the military from Portsmouth.

DORKING HIGH STREET

Scene of the "Swing Riots"

VICTORIA (1819) 1837-1901

The nineteenth century changed the face of Surrey dramatically and extensively. It is difficult to look around anywhere without being in debt to the Victorians. Practically every community has commemorated the Queen and Prince Albert somehow, from horse troughs to hospitals.

Architecturally, the most dramatic must be the Royal Holloway Sanatorium at Virginia Water. Perched on its ridge, silhouetted against the setting sun, it makes a most memorable skyline (above). Opened in 1884, it brings Europe to Surrey with this copy of the Cloth Hall at Ypres. The immitation Gothic should be no surprise as the architect, W.H.Crossland, was a pupil of Sir George Gilbert Scott. However, his companion building nearby, the Royal Holloway College, was inspired by the French renaissance style of Chateau Chambord and produces another striking building. They are claimed to be two of the greatest High Victorian buildings in Britain. Thus Queen Victoria didn't just open one of the first women's colleges in the country but also a monument to enterprise and endeavour, especially of the financier, Thomas Holloway, who made his name selling pills.

The search for royal servants has produced some surprises, not least the taxidermist to Queen Victoria. It was he who was responsible for this little stuffed dog that is now to be seen in Weybridge Museum. It is one of the Maltese Toy Dogs that were bred by the Dowager Duchess of Wellington when she was living at the Burhill Estate at Hersham. It was unfortunately run over by the coachman on a bicycle.

Of all the plants that we could grow to remind us of Queen Victoria perhaps lavender should head the list. Victoria was a great enthusiast of lavender. It was grown for her in Surrey in fields now swallowed up by the London Brough of Sutton and therefore outside the scope of this book. However the lavender stems, once harvested had to be sent to distilleries to extract the oil. Some of the Surrey harvest was sent to distilleries at Leatherhead.

In winter Chobham heath has the beauty of desolation. The scene in summer mellows in sharp contrast. Here on June 21st 1853 came Queen Victoria to review her troops. A cross was erected at the viewing point (map reference 965656) by 400 parishioners in 1901 to mark her death.

In 1858 it wasn't safe for her to review her troops at Aldershot due to an outbreak of cholera. Instead they paraded at Puttenham. The spot on Frosbury Hill was marked with a flagpole but it blew down in 1869. To commemorate Elizabeth II the site was restored in 1953.

This is a corner of Wanborough Manor House where Queen Victoria came as a guest of the tenant, Sir Algernon West. He was Parliamentary Private Secretary to Gladstone who also came as guest. He held Cabinet meetings here and wrote his farewell speech here. In order that such important guests could arrive with greatest ease he arranged for the building of Wanborough station, opened in 1891. This was possible because West was the Director of the railway company.

EDWARD VII
(1841) 1901-1910

Driving through Bagshot doesn't give one the impression that it has much history let alone be a royal place, but head for the stone-spired parish church on the hill. The interior is much more attractive than the outside. The west window is a memorial to Queen Victoria and includes her royal heraldry in the glass.

The east window was given by Edward and his brothers and sisters. The inscription reads, in part :- "To the Glory of God and in Loving Memeory of their dear brother Leopold George Duncan Albert, Duke of Albany K.G. Born April-7-1853. Died March-28- 1884." That was the year this church was built. The window, showing the Crucifixion, suffered from a flying bomb in the war so the present one is a copy of the original.

The window lights two tablets on the north wall. One reads :- "In loving memory of Major General HRH Prince Arthur of Connaught K.G.. Born at Windsor Castle 13th January 1883. Died in London 12th September 1938. This tablet was placed here by his wife, Princess Arthur of Connaught, Duchess of Fife."

The next one reads :- "In loving memory of Field Marshall HRH Arthur, Duke of Connaught and Strathearn K.G. Born at Buckingham Palace 1st May 1850. Died at Bagshot Park 16th January 1942. This tablet was placed here by his daughter, Lady Patricia Ramsay (Princess Patricia of Connaught)".

The Duke's splendid royal banner in red and gold hangs on the wall above. Two sanctuary candlesticks below are in memory of the servant who was comptroller to the Duke for eighteen years.

Turning round, the front pews are still carpeted in royal blue. Here the royal family sat when attending service. The same carpet occurs again in the pews of the north aisle. Here sat other members of the royal household.

An inscription on the back of the vestry door "placed here by parishioners 1948" records that in the last years of his life the Duke used this doorway to proceed to Holy Communion".

Bagshot Park still exists. A much clearer picture of the age can be gained from a visit to Polesden Lacey (National Trust) where Edward was entertained by Mrs Greville. There are lots of interesting photographs on display of the guests to the great house, including royalty. Other photographs extend our view. Matthew Alexander's "Guildford As It Was" includes one of the proclamation of Edward as king on January 31st 1901. Also included are scenes of Guildford decorated for his visit, as Prince of Wales, to open the Bath and West of England Show at Shalford Park on May 31st 1871.

The ancient traditions of hunting in the Surrey landscape were continuing. The wild cranes that gave their name to Cranleigh, were no longer coming. The herons, another delicacy of old, were out of fashion but pheasants were still a prime target. "The Shoot" became a major social occasion, not missed by Edward.

Henley Park (not open to the public) continued its own traditions of hosting royalty. Here, among other Surrey places, came Edward for sporting weekends. On December 5th 1900 he commemorated his visit in the usual way by planting a tree. It's now over fifty feet high.

Pheasants still abound in Surrey to remind us of those days. They're still hunted too. Out in the woods there are overgrown thickets of Rhododendron, (R. ponticum was introduced in 1763) and snowberry, Symphoricarpos albus, (introduced 1817) both of which were grown to provide cover for the game.

The Rue is one of our oldest garden plants, having been introduced by the Romans. It has Surrey connections with the improved cultivar "Jackman's Blue" and royal connections too. Edward's son, who became George V, was bestowed with the Order of the Rautenkrone (Crown of Rue) by the King of Saxony in 1902. It has been an armorial plant since the 12th century and incorporated in the collar of our Order of the Thistle since the 17th century.

Rue
2·7·85

Cock Pheasant
New Haw
25-5-1985

83

GEORGE V

(1865)
1910 ~ 1936

Epsom was all a bustle on June 4th 1913 for it was Derby Day. Up on the Downs all eyes and cameras were on the horses rounding Tattenham Corner. Suddenly a woman broke out of the crowds, rushed onto the course and throwing her arms up, was run down by the king's horse.

Police Constable F. Bunn was on duty at Tattenham Corner and although he saw her rush forward she was too quick for him. By the time he reached her she was quite unconscious. She was taken by motor car to Epsom Cottage Hospital.

Later she was identified as Miss Emily Wilding Davison, aged thirty eight from Long Horsley, Northumberland. "The horrid woman was injured but not seriously" wrote Queen Mary. Her sympathies were with "Poor Jones", the jockey, who "was much knocked about."

Emily was seriously injured though. She died on Sunday 8th June. Two days later the inquest was held by the West Surrey Coroner, Gilbert H. White, at Epsom Courthouse. The verdict was "Death by Misadventure". History books choose to call it suicide.

It is probably the best known event from Surrey's royal history after Magna Carta. That is largely due to it occuring in the age of photography when it made dramatic newsreel. She gets a brief mention in history books because, as her half-brother told the inquest, she was a "militant suffragist". He thought she did what she did to attract attention to the suffrage movement.

The king was not pleased. He had no sympathy for public disorder nor for the women's suffrage movement and certainly not when they both came together. He did have compassion though for people. He was, for example, concerned about the suffering inflicted by the methods of forced feeding exacted upon imprisoned suffragettes on hunger strike.

The 'Women's Movement' had been under way for some time. One starting point was Mary Wollstonecraft's "Vindication of the Rights of Women" published in 1792. The suffragettes arose from the failure (1886-1911) of J.S.Mill to get a bill passed giving the franchise to women. To a section of the female population it was granted in 1918.

The scene of the incident can still be visited today and of course the Derby is still run and Tattenham Corner is still there. Even the scene of such a recent story has changed though. The grandstand that is such a focal point of the great rolling landscape is not the one seen by Emily Davison. These buildings have all been renewed. Even the oldest part dates from the year after the above incident. The "Derby Arms" behind the buildings has a large portrait of the first Derby winner painted on its front elevation. That at least takes us back to earlier times.

N.B. Several reference books have spelt Emily's surname Davidson which can make her difficult to trace.

The Derby Arms.
Epsom Downs.
9.3.85.

The Derby began in 1780 (George III's reign) and was named after the Earl of Derby. He had already given the name of his house, "The Oaks" to the race founded the year before. Epsom had been a centre of horse racing for generations. Support from Cromwell, followed by Charles II, coupled with the discovery of salt springs ("Epsom Salts") in 1618 boosted the importance of Epsom into a spa town competing with Tunbridge Wells. James II and Queen Anne both visited. Victoria and Albert were present when W. McDonald won on "Little Wonder" which had begun at 50-1. Albert was so impressed with his beating the hot favourite by half a length that he presented him with a fine riding whip.

A more secluded corner of Surrey than Epsom Downs is the village of Elstead, with its medieval church and bridge, old cottages and mill, where the heathland comes down to the valley of the Wey. George V came here to review the troops on Hankley Common during the First World War. We can still follow his route today. He changed his car for a horse at the church and took the side lane down the hill to Westbrook, a delightful hamlet of cottages among the trees. The lane leads on through grassy spaces and trees to Hankley Common.

Hankley Common.

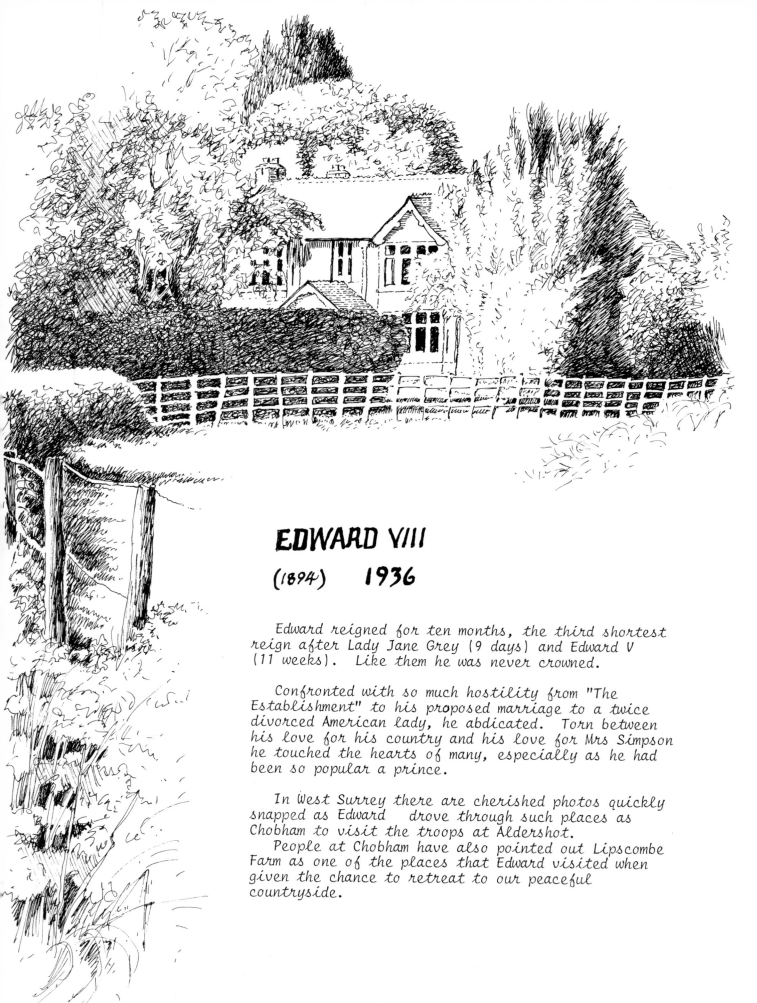

EDWARD VIII
(1894)   1936

Edward reigned for ten months, the third shortest reign after Lady Jane Grey (9 days) and Edward V (11 weeks).   Like them he was never crowned.

Confronted with so much hostility from "The Establishment" to his proposed marriage to a twice divorced American lady, he abdicated.   Torn between his love for his country and his love for Mrs Simpson he touched the hearts of many, especially as he had been so popular a prince.

In West Surrey there are cherished photos quickly snapped as Edward drove through such places as Chobham to visit the troops at Aldershot.
People at Chobham have also pointed out Lipscombe Farm as one of the places that Edward visited when given the chance to retreat to our peaceful countryside.

Wisley Gardens

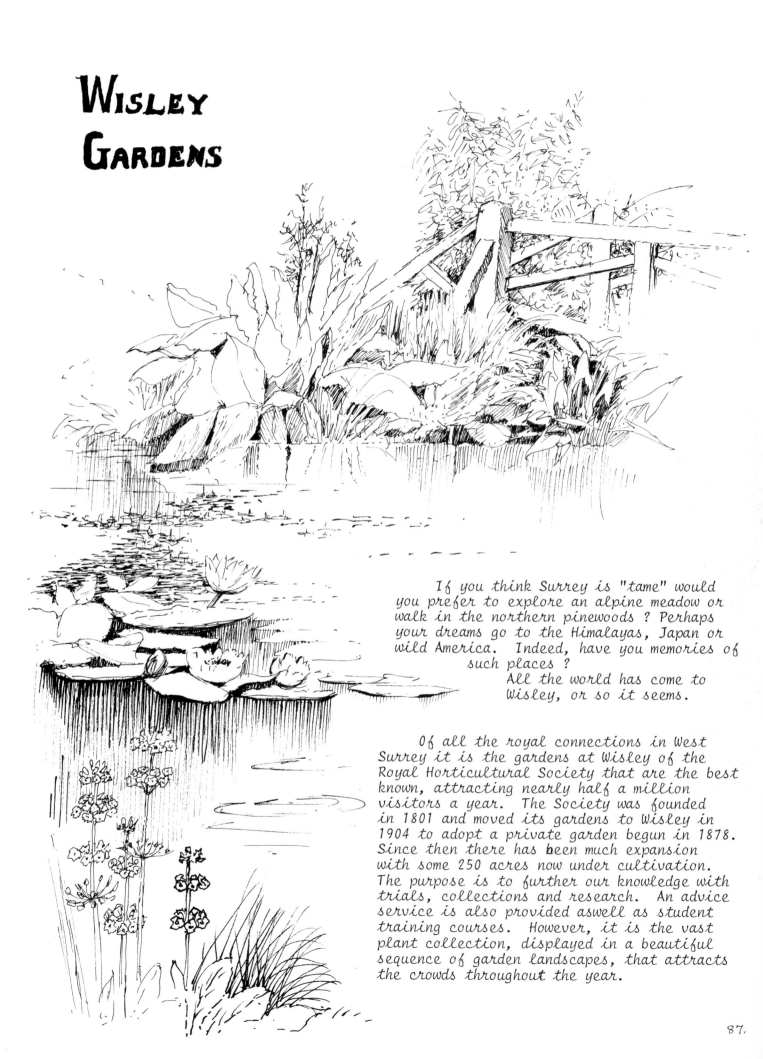

If you think Surrey is "tame" would you prefer to explore an alpine meadow or walk in the northern pinewoods ? Perhaps your dreams go to the Himalayas, Japan or wild America. Indeed, have you memories of such places ?

All the world has come to Wisley, or so it seems.

Of all the royal connections in West Surrey it is the gardens at Wisley of the Royal Horticultural Society that are the best known, attracting nearly half a million visitors a year. The Society was founded in 1801 and moved its gardens to Wisley in 1904 to adopt a private garden begun in 1878. Since then there has been much expansion with some 250 acres now under cultivation. The purpose is to further our knowledge with trials, collections and research. An advice service is also provided aswell as student training courses. However, it is the vast plant collection, displayed in a beautiful sequence of garden landscapes, that attracts the crowds throughout the year.

GEORGE VI
(1895)
1936 ~ 1952

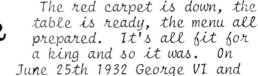

Coinage hasn't been considered so far but many people still have coins from this century, saved when decimal currency officially began on "D Day", 15th February 1971. During the reign of George VI two of the most popular were the farthing and the threepenny bit.

Except after severe winters the bushy places in Surrey are full of the popular little wren. Nearly our smallest bird, it featured on the smallest coin, the farthing and in this reign was minted until 1948. It had first been issued over 600 years earlier, by Edward I.

Those that were ready minted with the date 1952 continued to be issued in the reign of Elizabeth II.

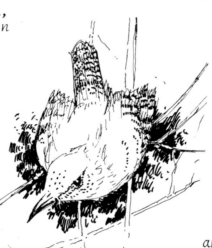

The threepenny bit, dodecagonal in shape, hasn't such a long history. It was first minted at York and London as part of the "fine coinage" issues of 1550-3.

It provides another chance to "grow your own history" for this coin featured "thrift", Armeria maritima. A popular rock garden plant, it can be seen in many Surrey gardens.

When Edward VIII abdicated in 1936 the mint had already produced his threepenny bits for the next year. These had to be melted down but just a few escaped.

The red carpet is down, the table is ready, the menu all prepared. It's all fit for a king and so it was. On June 25th 1932 George VI and Queen Elizabeth entered the room to take their places at the table. That moment of anticipation has been recreated by the National Trust and awaits the visitor at Polesden Lacey today. The menu for that day is on the table for all to read.

The room was already known to the royal couple for they had been lent the house for part of their honeymoon in 1923. They came on 26th April and stayed until 7th May; a time when the Corylopsis is covered with tassels of soft yellow flowers in one of the walled gardens and the Clematis armandii flowers on the south wall of the house. The more natural areas are full of English flowers: anemones and celandines, daffodils and wood spurge, cowslips and violets. To the great garden the royal couple added two blue spruces, near a copper beech planted by Edward VII in 1909. To Polesden Lacey George V and Queen Mary also came. Photographs of the royal guests and other distinguished visitors can be seen about the house, especially in the drawing room.

This is one of the most popular of the properties administered by the National Trust, with some 120 000 visitors a year.

The Royal Horticultural Society's gardens at Wisley were visited by the king and queen to officially open Aberconway House. This is a hostel for the students in residence at Wisley during their formal training for qualifications in horticulture. A tulip tree was planted to commemorate this occasion.

In 1964 Queen Elizabeth the Queen Mother came again to unveil the Bowes Lyon Pavilion, in memory of her brother Sir Edward Bowes Lyon KCVO. He had been president of the Royal Horticultural Society from 1953 until his death in 1961. On this occasion two upright tulip trees were planted.

Polesden Lacey ~ a glimpse into the dining room (blinds down).
Drawn by special arrangement
through the generosity of the National Trust.

27·5·85

ELIZABETH II
(1926) 1952 →

The bishop of Winchester features prominently through Surrey's history but in 1927 his vast diocese was divided into three, creating a new diocese of Guildford for much of Surrey. Thus in 1936 work began on a new cathedral, first envisaged by Henry VIII in 1534. The architect had been chosen by competition in 1934 and was Sir Edward Maufe. Eventually, despite war, the building was ready for consecration by the bishop, the Right Reverend George Reindorp, on May 17th 1961. The ceremony took place in the presence of the head of the Church of England, Her Majesty Queen Elizabeth II with His Royal Highness, Prince Philip. The dedication to The Holy Spirit was unique for an English Cathedral.

In 1977 the County joined the rest of the country in celebrating the Queen's Silver Jubilee and each place has its own memories of that occasion. Tucked away at Hydon Heath, Mr.A.George was persevering with breeding new hybrids for small gardens from Rhododendron yakushimanum. In this year a splendid new seedling first flowered. It was white with crimson lines in its throat and was christened "Silver Jubilee" - a lasting memorial to the reign and especially appropriate when the success of rhododendrons in Surrey would make it a contender for the 'County Flower'.

By now royal power is vastly different from that exercised where this book began. Nevertheless Her Majesty is still head of the church, the armed services and the judiciary. Her power lies not so much in what she does but in what she deprives **other** people from being able to do.

Guildford Cathedral
2·6·85
Sketched from 'The Oval'
Onslow Village

If you still get as confused as I do
with the correct order of some of our
kings and queens perhaps this old school
rhyme will help. You'll have to finish it
for yourselves though!

Willie, Willie, Henry, Stee,
Henry, Dick, John, Henry Three,
One, two, three Neds, Richard Two,
Henry Four, Five, Six, then who?
Edward Four, Five, Dick the Bad,
Henries twain and Ned the Lad,
Mary, Bessie, James the Vain,
Charlie, Charlie, James again,
William and Mary, Anna Gloria,
Four Georges, William, and Victoria;
Edward Seven came next and then
George the Fifth in 1910.

ACKNOWLEDGEMENTS

Collecting, selecting and presenting the material in this book has been made immeasurably easier with all the help given so willingly by friends and strangers. So it's a big THANK YOU to everyone, whether they contributed to the text, came out on location or asked basic questions which helped to keep the text from being too specialised. Unfortunately there hasn't been room to include all the results.

Once again I should like to thank Mrs. Bridget Harper and Mr. Paul Larkin of Chertsey Museum for their excellent service and encouragement for yet another book. Thanks also to Mrs. Avril Lansdell, Curator of Weybridge Museum, for permission to work from material in her care. The staffs of the museums at Dorking, Farnham and Guildford have also patiently given their time and knowledge.

Surrey County Library has been invaluable and the staffs at Weybridge, Leatherhead and Guildford need thanking in particular.

For help with some of the properties featured thanks are due to Miss Lyn Purvis, Vokes Ltd., Henley Park; the Master of the Hospital of the Blessed Trinity, Guildford; the Rev. P. Bus and Dr. D. Normanton for access to Old Woking and Bagshot churches; the guides at Loseley; officers of the National Trust, especially Mr. John Vandeleur Boorer, House Manager at Polesden Lacey, and his Senior Custodian, Mr. Glyn Fricker; officers of the Royal Horticultural Society, especially Mr. C. Brickell and Mr. B. Ambrose; and the custodian of Farnham Castle. Especially generous and hospitable were the owners of private properties.

Members of Local History Societies and readers of the Surrey Advertiser also provided assistance, as did Joanne Bradley, Mr. D. Howcroft, Mr, N. Hookins, Mr. G. Collyer and Mr. A. George, Rhododendron Specialist, Hydon Nursery.

Finally, thanks to Miss Anne Bawtree for proof reading.

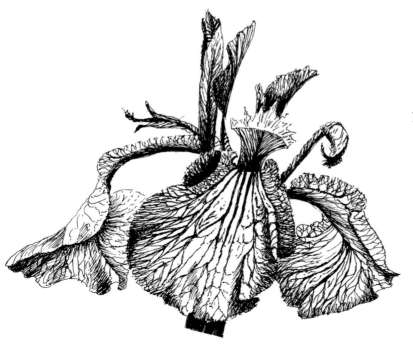

Iris flower which is thought to have given rise to the fleur-de-lis design used by English royalty since early in the 11th century. It was dropped from the Royal Arms about 1800.

INDEX OF PLACES
(Excluding those outside the
area covered in the book.)

Top: Surrey from the Jubilee Arboretum, R.H.S. Wisley; planted to mark Silver Jubilee of
Elizabeth II.

Virginia Water

"A kestrel for a knave" –
the bird rated lowest in
medieval falconry – the
sport of kings.

QUICK REFERENCE

Main entry in text underlined.

Gothic Revival scupture of a
king's head from Westcott church
built by Sir George Gilbert Scott
in 1852.